STRATEGIES FOR CATS

Change the Way You Think.
Receive the Abundance You Deserve!

Bill A Johnston

STRATEGIES FOR CATS. Change the Way You Think.
Receive the Abundance You Deserve!
Copyright © 2016 by Bill A Johnston

ISBN: 978-0-9972745-0-9

Library of Congress Control Number: 2016902000

The publisher has strived to be as accurate and complete as possible in the creation of this book.

This book is not intended for use as a source of legal, business, accounting, or financial advice. All readers are advised to seek services of competent professionals in legal, business, accounting, and financial fields.

In practical advice books, as in anything else in life, there are no guarantees of income made. Readers are cautioned to rely on their own judgment about their individual circumstances and to act accordingly.

While all attempts have been made to verify information provided for this publication, the publisher assumes no responsibility for errors, omissions, or contrary interpretation of the subject matter herein. Any perceived slights of specific persons, peoples, or organizations are unintended.

A Special Bonus from Bill

I am so thankful and grateful you have a copy of Strategies for Cats! It is my sincere hope that, by reading this book, you change the way you think so you can receive the abundance you deserve!

To express my gratitude, I'd like to give you a free, beautiful PDF featuring the 22 Strategies for Cats. It's a convenient and easy way to review and remember all the Strategies, and perfect for your refrigerator door!

To receive your free copy of the 22 Strategies for Cats suitable for framing, please visit our website:

http://www.strategiesforcats.com/bookbonus

To contact me for speaking engagements on Strategies for Cats, visit:

http://www.billajohnston.com

Plus, for even more on the book, the adventures of Kitty, and me, visit and <u>like</u> our Facebook page:

http://www.facebook.com/strategiesforcats

Dedication

For Cecelia, Mom, Dad,

Jennifer, Phillip, Matthew, Hudson, Weston, Max, Cecelia

Lightning, Puppy, Ayerston, and Kitty

Table of Contents

Introduction

The Power Cats Have Over People

Eleven years ago my wife Cecelia, our daughter Jennifer, and son Phill, lived in a lovely neighborhood in Northwest Greensboro, North Carolina. Our home was a large, tall two-story Colonial on a big hill.

Life was good!

In late November a stray feral cat began hanging around our house because a couple of people I lived with decided to feed it. I, however, chose to ignore their compassionate efforts, refused to listen to their conversations about "the poor cat" and how "cold it was outside." I tried not to care.

We already had three dogs, a Basset Hound, a Miniature Dachshund, and a Rat Terrier. In my mind, they had plenty of control over me already, dragging me down the stairs, taking them outside at all hours of the day *and* night so they can "do their business" and get a treat. Adding a cat would mean another animal manipulating me, another animal needing to be fed, another animal that has to go outside and do its business.

Oh wait…KITTY LITTER…and you know what that smells like! Who's going to clean that mess up?

SO…Why? WHY would we want another animal in our home? In the 20-year history of our family, we had never owned a cat. Why now? Why couldn't it just magically go away, find a home on its own…something else besides an outcome being us taking care of it for the rest of its life?

We named her "Kitty."

How was it possible a full grown man with a college education, successful career, the ability to drive a zoom machine (car) and a brain, be persuaded into adopting a homeless cat? Are all cats *really* that smart? Do they have this power over people where everything has to be their idea? Whether or not they'll let you pet them, feed them, or even adopt them?

You would think after being with us for these eleven years, and now that she's an indoor cat, she could be loving member of the family, but she won't sit in my lap, won't let me pick her up. When she does let me pet her, I have about a twenty percent chance of being bitten or scratched. Even now, I truly believe if Kitty was big enough, she would eat me.

The Secret.

The year we rescued and made Kitty a part of our family, Cecelia and I saw Oprah Winfrey get so excited about a DVD her friends were talking about, a DVD created by Rhonda Byrne called "The Secret" (Byrne, The Secret, 2006), a story about the "The Law of Attraction." Coincidentally, later that year we had access to the movie and watched it over and over again. I got so excited I started to research the people in the movie including Bob Proctor, Jack Canfield, and Joe Vitale. I bought their books, listened to their audio books, and because of Bob Proctor saying he reads Napoleon Hill's book "Think and Grow Rich" (Hill, 1937) every day, I thought I would do that too. What an amazing book.

It was also around this time my friend Dr. Gary Bradt, Speaker, Author, and Executive Coach on Change, encouraged me to become a professional speaker too. When I asked "how," we decided I needed to write a book. So I started writing!

For my first book, "The 10 Ways to Make Something Out of Nothing," I probably let twenty or so people read it.

My second one, a story about a homeless cat being adopted by us (the core of this book), I let another 5 read. Nobody was encouraging me to go further, but because of Gary's suggestion, and what Napoleon Hill describes as, "a definiteness of purpose" (Hill, 1937), I was not going to be defeated.

In 2013 I found a book written in the early 1960's by Joseph Murphy called, "The Power of your Subconscious Mind" (Murphy, 2007). It helped me understand the connection between The Law of Attraction, the way I think, and why "thoughts become things" (Byrne, The Secret, 2006). Then, after listening to an audio book by Joe Vitale called "Instant Manifestation: The Real Secret to Attracting What You Want Right Now (Vitale, 2011), I started thinking about my homeless cat book again, that maybe cats *do* have power over people because they instinctively know how to get what they want. It was then the creative part of my brain, my subconscious mind, created the title "Strategies for Cats."

It's the movie, the two books, Dr. Gary Bradt, my subconscious mind, my content editor Marie Snider, and my publishing mentor Diana M. Needham that all motivated me to write, write, rewrite, then finish this book.

When you read it, it is my sincere desire you discover you have an amazing and powerful subconscious mind, and you learn how to "team up" with it to get what <u>YOU</u> want. In this book we call it, "The Voice." By understanding this, learning this, believing this, "Strategies for Cats" will change the way you think so you can receive the abundance you deserve!

AND…I encourage you…to rescue a homeless cat!

Our story begins with our cat, "Kitty," in a storm drain across the street from our tall house. It's Thanksgiving time when everything's getting colder, and she *really* needs a place to live before Frosty Time (winter) comes.

Chapter 1: The Little Voice

Every neighborhood seems to have a homeless feral cat. You know, the kind that looks lonely, seemingly asking for human companionship with just the slightest glance. Yet when people approach the poor thing to give it a little love, it invariably stops dead in its tracks, flashes a startled look filled with fear, then bolts for the nearest hiding place.

Our cat is like any other feral cat, starting life at a disadvantage, born behind a bush or under a porch, taught to fend for herself, and never trust people. She's homeless; living by herself in a storm drain. If you asked her why she ended up there, she couldn't remember.

As the sun rises over the beautiful neighborhood of tall houses, look deep in her storm drain. See those two eyes glowing back at you? It's our cat, sitting on a perch high enough to see everything happening outside, like newly fallen leaves swirling in the air when the big yellow zoom machine drives by. She's wondering why the sun's coming up later, then going down earlier, making every night just a little bit colder and for a little longer.

Something is telling her Frosty Time is coming, the season when homeless cats should find a warmer place to live or die in an ice storm. But that's not what's on her mind.

She's hungry. The reality is she's *always* hungry.

"What cha thinking about, kitten?" It was the rat, a disgusting low-life, who lives in the sewer pipes with his no-good friends.

"Don't call me kitten," she snapped. "I'm a cat!"

"Oh yea," replied the rat with a slow southern drawl. "I keep forgettin'. Yea...uh...you're a...a cat. Right, right, right. Hey...uh...by the way, wadn't it coooold last night kitten...err I mean...cat? I'll bet cha was freezing ya little bottom off, sittin' on that 'tin little perch, shiverin' and shakin.' 'Course, I didn't have no problem 'cause it's warm down here-a. Why...you should be down here-a too! Ya know...with the rest of us...when it gets cold like that."

"I'm not coming down there," she quipped. "You just want to eat me."

"Oh no...never, never, never," the rat slyly assured her. "Why...we have the utmost respect for ya, kitten...uh...cat."

Sensing the need to change the subject, lest he get caught with what he was really thinking, the rat finally blurted, "YEP. It's getting coooooolder. When Frosty Time gits here, you'll have to git outta here-a."

Suddenly he was inspired by a fantastic idea. "Hey…why don't ya just trot over the hill? There's a big 'ol cat named Jim livin' there. I've heard tell he's pretty nice! Maybe he'll let ya live *there* during Frosty Time. And just lookin' at how big he is, I'm *shore* he's got plenty of food to fill that growlin' belly of yours."

Of course, the rat knew Big Jim was known to fight cats crazy enough to trespass on his turf. If she takes his suggestion, our cat could get killed. IT WAS A BRILLIANT PLAN! The thought of a dead cat made the rat salivate.

"I've never met another cat before," she anxiously said. "Do you think it'll be okay? Do you really think he'll help me?" As she asked the rat question after question, she wondered why a rodent that she knows deep her heart wants to eat her, would try to help her stay alive. It was confusing, but the lure of staving off hunger *and* finding a warm place was too enticing. It blinded her instincts.

"Don't ya worry about a thing, kitten," the rat said confidently. "Big Jim lives with people who have plenty of room in their tall, tall, *tall* house. What's more-a…who could resist a dear-a like yooo?"

In the meantime, a little voice inside our cat was nudging her, telling her danger was on the other side of the hill. But she ignored it. The temptation was far too great for her to listen.

She emerged from the storm drain, checked to be sure the coast was clear, calmly took a seat on top of the brown round thing, then looked up the hill to imagine meeting Big Jim. What would it be like to meet him? Would he be nice to her? Help her? So many questions!

As she pondered the idea, her tail was pounding the brown round thing so hard it made a small clanging sound that echoed in the cavern below. Then she looked down the hill toward the empty field. She calls it the empty field for a reason. There are barely enough mice to keep her alive. That's why she is always hungry. As she turned away, her little voice nudged her again. It was answering her question, what could happen if she meets Big Jim, telling her danger was on the other side of the hill. She still wasn't listening.

But then she made a BIG DECISION. In the blink of an eye, she started racing up the hill. "I wonder if Big Jim's people have lots of food," she thought excitedly. "Will they give me a warm place to live during Frosty Time? Will Big Jim help me? I wonder..."

More questions flew through her head until suddenly she was at the top of the hill. She slowed and thought to herself, "Wow, I've never been here before. Look at all the tall houses, the trees, everything. It's so beautiful!"

She paused to take in the splendor then slowly began trotting down the hill. As she did, she was getting closer to answering the question about Big Jim.

Then…he appeared.

She could see him, a huge, white and black cat in a yard just a few more tall houses down the hill. "That must be him," she thought. "That's gotta be Big Jim."

Big Jim was basking in the morning sun, lying on his full belly. His oversized head was bobbing up and down ever so slightly, while the tip of his tail occasionally tapped the luscious green grass. He looked like he was plucking aromas out of the air, enjoying them like fine caviar. His eyes were closed, shielding the blinding glow radiating from his fur.

But THEN…there was an aroma that wasn't so fine, an aroma he didn't like. He opened his eyes, and staring back at him was our cat. SHE WAS IN HIS FACE!

"Hi," she said excitedly.

Big Jim quickly stood. He was huge. "WHO ARE YOU?" he demanded.

"Oh…um…HI!" she said nervously. "I'm a cat from the other side of the hill! I'm cold at night. It's getting colder…and…um…I'm always hungry…yea…hungry…anyway…"

Big Jim was pissed! He stared at our cat for what felt like an eternity, then sternly responded. "You see the door over there?" Jim angrily motioned toward a little door on the front of the zoom machine door. "When I'm hungry, I go in the door. When I'm cold, I go in the door. If it's raining, I go in the door. And see the name on the door? It's my name. JIM! That means it's MINE!"

"You are so lucky," she said, "having all those things, plus you even have a name." Then she sighed. "I wish I had a name. Will the people give me a name? Will they put my name next to your name so I can go in the door too?"

When our cat finished talking, she stood straight up on the tips of her paws, lifted her tail, slightly cocked her little head, closed her eyes then made a loving move toward Big Jim. A HUGE mistake!

WHACK!

Big Jim swiped the claws on his left paw across our cat's right cheek. When she opened her eyes, red dots were floating everywhere!

WHACK! WHACK! WHACK!

Three more smacks, this time from Big Jim's right paw. Streaks of blood emerged from her cheeks. Then, as if his rage had no boundaries…

BIG JIM JUMPED HER!

The sheer weight of Big Jim forced her legs buckle, flattening her empty stomach to the ground. As he mightily positioned himself on her back, her claws were desperately clutching the grass. She couldn't move. Big Jim slowly opened his mouth, revealing long, white fangs of death then inserted them in our cat's tiny neck with amazing strength!

MEEEEEEOOOOOOOOOWWWWWWW!

Her shrill cry was so loud a man and a woman rushed from the house toward the cats. Big Jim knew if he kept fighting, he could lose their love *and* everything they gave him behind the door…HIS door…so he quickly climbed off our cat's back then cowardly feigned his own injury. What an evil manipulator!

When our cat stood, the blood flooding her eyes dripped uncontrollably to the ground. More blood, spewing from her neck, revealed just how skinny she really was. There was so much it turned her grey fur to red!   Her instincts were telling her to flee, but where!? She was totally disoriented, had no sense of direction, couldn't see, and was just about to faint.

THEN…something happened that cannot be explained. She heard a soft, deep voice, but she didn't hear it with her ears. It was a voice in her head! It was a voice in her head, and it was talking to her!

"RUN!" the voice said. "RUN AWAY!"

Our cat didn't know what to do, so she waited…waited to hear the voice again. Was the voice really coming from her head? She couldn't make out a face because she was fighting through the blood.

"RUN!" the voice said. "RUN AWAY!"

She took off like a bolt of lightning, but as her frail body reached the crest of the hill, she became light headed, then while bounding down the hill, panic set in. She lost her footing and fell.

"UGH!"

Her head lunged into the ground. The force was so physically powerful it pushed the little ball in her neck deep into her throat. When she landed, her body slid on its side, leaving a bright red streak of blood on the grass.

"Get up!" the voice said. "GET UP AND **GO**!"

She leapt to her feet like she was raised by the hand of Big Cat, but began to stumble, her left side leading her right, ready to fall again. Then…SHE MADE IT! She crawled in the storm drain and collapsed on her perch.

As she tried to catch her breath, she sensed she wasn't alone. The rats were filling the floor beneath her, squeaking with glee!

"My word, kitten," the rat said, pretending to act astonished. "Why look at ya…all bloodied up. Why…it's just a shame to see ya like this. Did Big Jim do this?"

The rats erupted with laughter.

It would be just a matter of moments before she would pass out, and fall off her perch. Then, it would be supper time!

The blood covering our cat turned black. Then her breathing changed. Instead of fast, heavy breaths, they began slowing down, getting shorter. It was then she *thought* to herself, "I want to live…I want to live…I want to live…I want to live…," but as her eyes closed, her head began to wobble. She couldn't hold it up. It fell to her blood drenched paws with a thud.

"Yes," the voice said. "Your wish is my command. Can you hear me? Can you hear me? CAN YOU HEAR ME?"

Our cat couldn't hear a thing. Her eyes closed, her mind fell into a dream, and then her body went limp. Soon she could be gone...

The miracle.

As our cat started to dream, her voice was getting busy. "She wants to live," the voice said, "I can make her dream come true. I will ask Big Cat for help."

Then the voice began to pray. "Big Cat, please...come into my heart. Give me the healing I need to return to life; and Big Cat, I am thankful for all you have given me and all that is coming. For this miracle, I am eternally grateful."

When darkness fell, the sky began shedding tears, so many tears they made a stream that flowed into our cat's storm drain like a raging river. The sound was roaring! Then...her miracle happened! Her little tail started to tap...the moist air melted the hardened blood off her fur...her heart began beating...her body was filling with new energy...and as she was healing...our cat was glowing!

Not only did she receive her miracle, she was given a rare gift. For now…for a while…she can hear herself think, because the voice, the voice she heard inside her head, is not going away anytime soon.

Strategy 1

Listen for the little voice.

When you feel a nudge, an idea comes to your head, or you even hear a little voice, it's your subconscious mind communicating with you.

Our cat heard the little voice, but didn't listen. Temptation has a wicked way of giving us less than what we dreamed.

She learned a hard lesson; a lesson that almost cost her life. But as she gets to know the voice, she'll start listening. And you should, too.

Chapter 2: Thoughts Become Things

As our cat wakes to start a new day, she doesn't remember everything about the fight with Big Jim, how she lost most of her blood from the fang holes in her neck, or the scratches across her face. Her miracle has left her so completely healed that the fight is not foremost on her mind.

No, she is not remembering all of yesterday because the overwhelming feeling she is waking up to is the same feeling she's had for as long as she can remember.

Hunger.

She's had nothing to eat for two days. Now it hurts.

As the big yellow zoom machine roars by her storm drain, she picks up her head to watch the plume of rustling leaves trailing behind. Then...she hears it.

"Good morning," the voice softly said.

"Is that you, rat?" she said weakly. "You knew Big Jim would hurt me. You were hoping he would....and I heard you and your slimy friends wanting to eat me last night...so just go away," she said, hurting like she lost the only friend she ever had. "Go away, rat, go away!"

"Good Morning," the voice said again.

Our cat blinked a long blink then looked down at the sewer pipe. The rat wasn't there. She looked outside the storm drain, wondering if the sound was from the street. Nobody was there, either.

Then she remembered the voice she heard in her head. "Who are you?" she anxiously asked.

"I…am…you," the voice said deliberately.

When dying cats come back to life, some of them get smarter. Maybe while they're healing they get so close to their voice, the voice working in the supernatural to keep them alive, when they finally do wake up, they are almost like one.

"Something must have happened after the fight with Big Jim," the voice said. "That's when you heard my voice. For some reason, you can still hear me. It must be a lingering part of the miracle you received."

"You are me?" our cat asked.

"Yes," the voice encouragingly said.

"Does that mean I'm talking to myself," she asked.

"Yes," the voice agreed. "All cats talk to themselves, but it is unusual their voice talks back. That is what is different…for now. It will end."

She was beginning to understand. "Was it *you* trying to tell me there was danger on the other side of the hill?"

"Yes," the voice said.

"I was asking *you* questions?" she asked.

"Yes," the voice said, "I have the answers for all of your questions."

You were asking about going to the other side of the hill, would Big Jim help you; would the people give you a warm place to live during Frosty Time. My answer was danger…there was danger on the other side of the hill."

"If you knew there was danger, why did you let me go?" she asked.

"I have the answers for all of your questions," the voice said.

"You made a *decision*. You decided to go."

"You let me go to the other side of the hill even though you knew there was danger?" she asked.

"Yes," the voice said.

"Why didn't you stop me?" she asked befuddled.

"I give you the answers," the voice said. "You make decisions."

"But it's so wrong!" she continued. "Wrong to do that…to let me…you…us…I mean me…almost get killed."

"Knowing the difference between wrong and right are decisions," the voice said. "I give you answers; you make decisions."

"How do I know you…are me?" she asked. "Maybe I'm just having a crazy dream."

The voice welcomed the challenge, because most cats will never know they have a voice:

- With the power to turn their thoughts into things.
- Dedicated to keeping them healthy and alive, including the ability to heal.
- Remembering and recording everything for future use.
- Always watching out for them day and night, even while they are sleeping.

Teaching our cat to know her voice is real, helping her learn to communicate with it, believing in her voice…in herself, would be a huge life-changing moment. Teaming up with her voice on purpose and becoming one with the voice, our cat would have the power to get anything she wanted to get, do anything she wanted to do, and be whoever she wanted to be.

"I was here before you were born," the voice confided. "I started your heart beat and I keep it going. Are *you* beating your heart on purpose?"

"No," she said.

"Your breathing," the voice stated. "Are you breathing on purpose?"

Thinking for a moment, she replied, "Sometimes I do, but maybe not all the time, like when I'm sleeping. You do that?" she asked.

"Yes," the voice said. "It's one of the thousands of things I do for you, *all* at the same time."

The voice was convincing our cat.

"You…are…me?" she asked again.

"Yes," the voice confirmed.

"You healed me," she said, "you answer my questions, you do thousands of things for me all the time"?

"Yes," the voice said.

"How can you help me?" she wondered.

The voice paused for effect, wanting to be sure our cat heard one of the most powerful things it can do.

"I can help you," the voice said. "I have the power to turn your thoughts into things."

"Thoughts?" she asked.

"Yes," the voice said. "I hear the thoughts you think about most and then manifest them into your physical life. If you <u>ask</u> for something, <u>believe</u> in me, believe so hard you have already received it, then you will <u>receive</u> it. I make your dreams and wishes come true."

Our cat has only one thing on her mind.

"What am I thinking about now?" she asked.

"Hunger," the voice said, "Hunger is your thought habit. You think about hunger when you wake up, you think about hunger before you sleep, and when your mind is blank hunger is your first thought. Yes, hunger is your thought habit."

"So…can you hear what I'm thinking about now?" she asked.

"Yes," the voice said.

"I **don't** want to be hungry," she shouted. "Can you make that thought into a thing?"

"Yes," the voice said. "What you think about is what I bring about."

Our cat was so enthused that she leapt off her perch, crawled out of the storm drain, and then darted across the street toward the empty field. She crept through the tall grass, jumped behind big rocks, snuck up on every hiding place she could remember. But after spending the entire morning not even finding one mouse, one disappointed feral cat retreated to her storm drain; tip toed onto her perch, then plopped down on her empty stomach.

"You said my thoughts become things," she said sarcastically.

"Yes," the voice replied confidently. "I brought you hunger."

"WELL THAT WAS WRONG!" she complained. "I told you I **don't** want to be hungry."

"I can tell by your anger you are unhappy," the voice patiently replied. "What do you think you are asking for?"

"I **DON'T** WANT TO BE HUNGRY!" she said sternly.

"Your thoughts are very clear," the voice confessed. "You want hunger."

Our cat was fuming now.

Breaking the standoff, the voice encouragingly said, "Here is an idea. Ask me again…for what you want. This time use different words."

"I WANT FOOD!" she screamed out loud. "I WANT TO EAT FOOD! I WANT MY BELLY TO BE FULL OF *FOOD*!"

"You want food," the voice said.

"Yes," she insisted, almost relieved. "Food! I want food!"

"Your wish is my command," the voice proclaimed. "Go to the empty field. Expect an abundance of food."

Once again our cat leapt from the storm drain with high expectations, this time with tremendous energy and a definiteness of purpose.

There were mice everywhere!

When the day ended she emerged from the empty field, only now she was practically tipsy. Our cat was full…of food! She strutted across the street, crawled into the storm drain, did a 360 on her perch, then collapsed.

For the first time ever, she was going to sleep full of food.

"Do you believe in me?" the voice asked.

Our cat couldn't comprehend the question. "Believe in you?" she asked. "What does that mean?"

"Do you believe it was me who provided you with an abundance of food?" the voice asked.

"Well…Yes," our cat conceded, "I asked for food, and you gave me food."

"Tomorrow…will there be an abundance of food in the empty field," the voice challenged, "or will it be an empty field, a field that reminds you of your thought habit, hunger?"

Our cat showed a blank look on her face.

"For as long as you can remember," the voice said, "your thought habit has been hunger, so hunger is what I have brought you. Now you wish to change your thought habit to food because food is what you've wanted all along."

"Will there be an abundance of food in the empty field tomorrow?" she asked.

"Yes," the voice said.

 "I have the answers for all of your questions," the voice said.

Pausing to let our cat understand, the voice said, "The answer is to change the way *you* think. Let the hunger feeling go, forget your hunger thought habit. Instead, every time the thought of hunger comes to your mind, replace it with a feel-good thought. Remember today, how you went into the empty field and discovered an abundance of food, how you feel now, full and fulfilled? *This* is your feel-good thought!"

Our cat was getting sleepy, so sleepy she let herself absorb everything the voice had to say without judgment. For the first time she was starting to feel good about life.

"At the end of your day," the voice softly whispered, "while you are falling asleep, I want you to think of this is as the best time to tell me what you want, to express gratitude for all you have been given, and for all you are about to receive."

Ask, Believe, Receive

As eyes are closing for a good night's sleep, the voice said, "Let us end our day with a lullaby, a lullaby to repeat when we go to sleep so we are thinking about good things, because when you think good thoughts, you get good things. For tonight, it's a lullaby about an abundance of food."

"What's a lullaby," our cat asked.

"A lullaby is a phrase you repeat over and over right before you go to sleep," the voice softly said. "A lullaby is when you <u>ask</u> for what you want, <u>believe</u> it is already yours then remember you have already <u>received</u> it. Are you ready?"

"Yes," she said, almost like the beginning of a purr, "I am ready."

"There's an abundance of food in the food field," the voice said. "There's an abundance of food in the food field. Say it."

"There's an abundance of food in the food field," our cat said.

"Keep going." the voice said. "Keep going until you are fast asleep."

There's an abundance of food in the food field.
There's an abundance of food in the food field.
There's an abundance of food in the food field.
There's an abundance of food in the food field.
There's an abundance of food in the food field.
There's an abundance ….
Purr…purr…purr…purr…

Strategy 2

Use your thoughts the right way to get the things you want.

Negative thoughts end with negative results. Our cat was constantly repeating "I don't want to be hungry," which means her *thought habit* was a negative thought. It was even more confusing to the voice because it does not understand the word "don't or do not," so it was hearing, "I want to be hungry."

By changing the words and expressing what she is for (not against); she is for food (and not against hunger), her voice worked immediately to fulfill the new request.

Before our cat could hear her own voice, they were working independently. The end result was hunger.

However, when they began to "team up," she discovered an abundance of food.

Ask…believe…and receive!

Strategy 3

When in doubt, ask your voice for the answer.

The greatest cats in history were known to ask their voice to answer their questions. Many times they would plant the question in their mind before going to sleep or prior to a cat nap.

If your voice doesn't have the answer to your question, it has the power to travel the universe, relentlessly sifting through billions and billions of thoughts "in the ether," until it finds your answer.

It may take time. Be patient. When your voice returns with the answer, you'll know it.

Chapter 3: Believe in Your Voice

When feral cats teach their kittens about survival, they implant an expectation of lack and scarcity, which relentlessly permeates the way they think for the rest of their lives. It's no different for our cat whose mother taught her what generation after generation had passed on to their young, that finding food is so hard you will always be hungry. Yet, for the first time ever, she is waking up without an aching tummy!

"I know what you're thinking," the voice said. "You remember hearing a voice in your head yesterday, but it had to be a dream because it ended so well."

Our cat was so sleepy that she didn't react. She just listened.

"The ache in your tummy is missing," the voice said, "yet your thought habit is still hunger."

As the voice was quietly nudging our cat, suddenly the big yellow zoom machine startled her as it roared by the storm drain. Leaves swirled into her cavern. She picked up her head in a panic, like she had been sleeping way too long. Was somebody trying to hurt her?

"It is okay," the voice said assuredly. "I am keeping you safe."

When our cat heard the calming voice, she closed her eyes and smiled. It was really happening! Then the voice asked, "Shall we return to the field and enjoy another feast?"

She thought it would be amazing if what happened yesterday happened again today. Saliva began to fill her mouth, as her thought habit was changing from hunger to abundance.

"Remember the lullaby I taught you before you fell asleep?" the voice asked. "Do it again. Close your eyes, tap your tail, say it…say your lullaby over and over again."

Our cat dutifully obeyed the voice. She dropped her head onto her front paws, closed her eyes, and began purring the food phrase, saying:

There's an abundance of food in the food field.
There's an abundance of food in the food field.
There's an abundance of food in the food field.
There's an abundance of food in the food field.
There's an abundance of food in the food field.
There's an abundance of food in the food field.
There's an abundance of food in the food field.
There's an abundance of food in the food field.

The voice interrupted her. "Okay, open your eyes. Tell me how you feel."

As our cat opened her eyes, she raised her head to gaze across the street toward the field formerly known as the empty field, now called the food field.

"I feel…" she was thinking, "I feel that when I go to the food field, I'll find food. I'll find food just like yesterday. Yep, I believe I'll find food."

"Good," the voice said. "Now…do you...believe in *me*?"

Our cat still didn't realize the magnitude of the question. In reality, the voice was asking if she believed in herself and her own ability to use her voice…her mind…to find food.

Without hesitation, she crawled out of her storm drain, quickly walked across the street with the same definite purpose as before, then just as she entered the food field, she paused to answer the voice. "Yes," she said. "I believe in you."

When she entered the food field, it was just as she left it. Food was everywhere!

Negative Nancy.

When our cat could eat no more, she paused to enjoy a totally satisfied feeling. But then she saw a cat coming toward her that she had never seen before. It wasn't a fine looking cat like Big Jim. This one was disheveled. Yellow was its main color with a few white spots. Even her tail was crooked.

Instinctively, our cat should have been skittish about meeting another cat. The last time she let her guard down there was danger, but this time her voice wasn't warning her.

"Howdy!" the yellow cat said with a welcoming voice. "There's no food in there, is there?"

"Actually, there is," our cat replied. "In fact, it's been a wonderful morning. I am stuffed."

"Well that's impossible," the yellow cat interrupted. "You must have been lucky. I never find food in there. It's like someone's conspiring to hide it from me. I don't even know why I bother."

The yellow cat was inspecting her body like she was looking for something. Then it dawned on her. "I know who you are," it said, "you had the cat fight with Big Jim, but I don't see any marks on you."

"Yea," our cat said, "They must have gone away when I was healed."

Not understanding what our cat just said, the yellow cat replied, "Why in the world would you mess with a typical male cat like Big Jim? They *all* act like they're better than we are."

Letting her guard down, our cat asked, "Is that why Big Jim was so mean to me, because he's a male cat?"

"Yea," the yellow cat confirmed. "He's a typical male, a beautiful house, people taking care of him, feeding him exotic foods, and keeping his kitty litter fresh. Did you see the door with his name on it? What an arrogant male!"

The yellow cat was very persuasive. "You're right," our cat agreed. "Why should a mean, male cat get all those nice things while I live in a storm drain? It's not fair."

"You poor little kitty, stuck in that old storm drain with absolutely nothing," the yellow cat agreed. "What's your name?"

Almost ashamed, she replied, "I don't have a name, I wish I did. How do you get one?"

"People give you a name," the yellow cat said sympathetically, "but you don't live with people. You'll probably never get one."

"Do you have a name," asked our defeated cat.

"Of course *I* have a name," the yellow cat said. "I'm Nancy."

"How does it feel to have a name?" our cat asked.

"Well...for me," Nancy said, "when I got my name, it made me feel like a part of their family. I guess it's because all the people in my family have names, too. But you'll have to figure out how to live with people to get a name, and that's nearly impossible, especially if you're a female *and* a feral cat."

Nancy was so negative that our cat forgot about the abundance she had just received from the voice. Instead, Nancy was making her feel bad.

"So…why *did* you go to Big Jim's?" Nancy asked.

"I'm worried about Frosty Time," our cat confided. "I need a warm place to live. But I didn't know I would be afraid of people, like the man and woman who came running toward me when Big Jim was biting my neck."

"Your scream was terrifying," Nancy said, "but you can't be afraid of people. People give you nice things like cat food and a safe place to sleep. I have a bed in the big room with the zoom machines. It's a little cold during Frosty Time. Of course, it would be much nicer if I was a male cat like Big Jim."

Nancy looked over our cat's shoulder toward the food field. "You're telling me you actually found food over there? You're kidding, right?"

"I'm not kidding," our cat said, remembering what she had just enjoyed. "It used to take me a whole day to find one measly mouse, but since my fight with Big Jim, I can hear a voice in my head. It taught me a cat lullaby. Now finding food is easy."

"A cat lullaby?" asked a doubting Nancy. "A voice in your head taught you a cat lullaby, and now you're finding food? HA! I don't believe it."

"You don't believe me?" our cat replied meekly. "You don't believe my cat lullaby worked?"

"No," Nancy said. "I think you took too many hits in the head from Big Jim, if you know what I mean," she said sarcastically.

"Well..." she challenged, "if the food phrase doesn't work, then how come *I* can find mice, and you can't?"

"How does it work?" Nancy asked judgmentally. "Do you even know? If you don't know *how* the lullaby works, then how could you possibly know...the lullaby worked?"

Our cat was speechless. She didn't know how to answer Negative Nancy because she didn't know how it works either. Sure, the last two times she entered the food field mice were everywhere, but hundreds of times before it *was* empty. Nancy had our cat starting to doubt her voice.

"If you don't know *how* something works, how do you know if *it's* working? Are you absolutely sure the mice came out because of this cat lullaby you learned about from some voice you heard where, in your head? Or do you think maybe, just maybe, you got lucky?"

Our cat still couldn't respond. Nancy's argument was winning her over.

"Do you *really* believe mice just come out of their holes so you can eat them because of a bunch of words you're singing to yourself?" Nancy asked. "What difference would it make?"

Nancy couldn't contain herself any longer. "Ha ha ha! You're a crazy cat, crazy for believing in such a thing. A cat lullaby...Ha ha ha!"

Nancy side stepped our cat, then bounded into the food field. "I'll prove there's no food in this field!"

As Nancy searched the food field, a doubting and dejected feral cat returned to her storm drain. After all, how *could* a bunch of words bring her an abundance of food?

"I still haven't found one," Nancy gleefully yelled from the field. She was experiencing great joy proving our cat wrong.

Despite having a belly full of food, her head filled with doubt.

"How *does* it work?" our cat thought to herself. "How does the cat lullaby work?"

As she crawled on her perch, the voice was silent. In the distance you could still hear Nancy. "I see nothing in here," she was shouting. "NOTHING!"

When in doubt, ask your voice for the answer.

The sun was setting. The voice was eerily silent since meeting Nancy, making our cat feel vulnerable and alone. She began shaking as the cold air was filling her cavern. Finally...a familiar sound returned to her head.

"You're confused," the voice softly stated. "Your day began filled with abundance, yet now you have doubts, doubts about me; about your miracle, why you can hear me, or if I even exist."

"Where have you been?" she asked like she was wounded. "I have been waiting to hear your voice."

"I…am…you," the voice replied. "I was here when you woke, with you when you leapt into the food field, when you experienced an abundance of food. When you met Nancy, *you*…forgot about *me. You*…let Nancy fill your head with doubts; doubts about me and the power of your lullaby."

After a pause, the voice softly said, "*You*…need to decide if you believe in me."

Our cat began her day saying she believed in her voice, but the question Nancy posed, the question she couldn't answer, was still a doubt.

"I think I believe in you," she confessed, "but how do you do what you do? How do you talk to me in my head? How does the cat lullaby work? How can a bunch of words bring me food?"

"I have the answers for all of your questions," the voice said.

There was silence. Our cat wondered if she said too much.

"Why do you have to know *how* something works to know that it does work?" the voice asked. "Life is easier and far more abundant if you simply believe the cat lullaby works then use it over and over again to enjoy an abundance of food."

"You don't have to know *how* it works?" she asked. "Was Nancy not telling me the truth?"

"Is there a reason you or Nancy or any other cat has to know how a thing works before you can use it or enjoy it?" the voice asked. "Does Nancy have to know how her ears work before she can hear? Does Nancy have to know how her eyes work before she can see? Does Nancy have to know how the sun works before she can enjoy its light and warmth?"

"No," our cat said, her head nodding up and down.

"Nancy could live a life filled with abundance," the voice counseled. "She has a voice just like you, with the same power to get whatever she wants. Unfortunately, her thought habit is lack and scarcity, which in her mind justifies why male cats get more than female cats, why some cats live in beautiful homes with the people, while she sleeps on the cold floor in the zoom machine room, why Big Jim looks so wealthy, and she looks so poor. Whatever Nancy thinks about, Nancy's voice brings about."

Our cat asked, "Is that why Nancy made fun of the cat lullaby?"

"Yes," the voice responded. "Cats like Nancy have a hard time believing in anything unless you can prove it to them. Plus…they are always the victim. They are always hungry. They are always poor. Their negative thoughts become their negative things. Is that what *you* want? Or would you prefer a life filled with abundance…and with food?"

"Food," our cat declared. "I want food."

"Have you made a decision?" the voice asked. "Do you believe in me?"

"Yes," our cat said. She was starting to get sleepy.

"Now," the voice quietly said, "at the end of this day…while you are sleepy, let's repeat your thankfulness and your gratitude for the abundance of food you are receiving.

As our cat closed her eyes, the memories of the day evaporated. She was so full of food, so content, she forgot the cold.

The voice said, "Tonight, we will change your lullaby to be you are so grateful and thankful for the abundance of food in the food field. Say it."

"I am so grateful…and thankful…for the abundance of food in the food field. I am so grateful…and thankful… for the abundance of food in the food field. I am so grateful…and thankful…purr purr…"

Strategy 4

Believe in your voice.

When you believe in your voice, and your voice hears your wants and wishes, you are on the same team. When it happens...when you "team up" with your subconscious mind, when you are working in concert, miracles can happen.

Strategy 5

You don't have to know how something works to make it work for you.

If you did, your life would be quite limited.

Strategy 6

Express gratitude for the abundance you are receiving.

When you are grateful and thankful for gifts, expressing gratitude, being thankful for what you have received has a way of attracting even more into your life. So always be grateful and express gratitude.

Strategy 7

Stay away from negative cats.

It's easy for poverty to make its way into your thoughts. Cats like Negative Nancy are everywhere. She set out to prove there was no abundance, there was no food, and the cat lullaby didn't work.

Thoughts become things.

In Nancy's mind, she thought there was nothing in the food field. What did she receive? Nothing.

Chapter 4: Good Vibrations

As the days go by you can tell our cat is enjoying the abundance of food in the food field by the way she looks. She's bigger. But the weather continues turning cold, making Frosty Time her new thought habit. She doesn't know what to expect, which is why the emotion of fear is penetrating her thinking. Fear of the cold, fear of the unknown, fear she will find herself full of food; then frozen to death. It's an image she can't get out of her mind.

She's also remembering her conversation with Nancy, wondering why a mean, selfish cat like Big Jim enjoys a warm place to live while she endures the cold and wet weather in a storm drain. It's not fair. It's not right. She has become envious.

The food field.

After a good night's sleep, our cat is exploring the food field. It's cold! It's so cold the vegetation is covered with a light layer of frost. It's so cold she can see her breath.

"The sun is out, and I'm still freezing," she complained.

"I am here for you," the voice said.

"Will it get colder than this?" she asked.

"Yes," the voice said calmly. "It will get colder. Frosty Time is brutal when you live outside."

"I don't want to live outside," our cat complained. She forgot how her voice has problems hearing some words.

"The image you always think about," the voice said, "of you, full and frozen, it is very powerful. You show it to me all the time, so I am making you bigger, growing your fur. I want to keep you alive."

As she looked at her legs, then peered over her shoulder to check her new growth, she asked "You're *seeing* what I'm thinking?"

"Yes," the voice said. "You see things with your eyes. I see what you are thinking…what you are visualizing…and because you are afraid, you are filling with fear…fear of the unknown. The combination is so powerful I *have* to manifest this in your material life."

Then our cat remembered how the voice doesn't hear all the words, how the voice works on her thoughts, that her thoughts become things.

"What I think about is what you bring about," our cat said.

"Yes," the voice agreed.

Our cat quickly shook her head a few times to clear her thoughts. She's trying to understand her voice.

"You are making me bigger," she said, "growing my fur, to keep me alive, and at the same time bringing me what I'm thinking about? Being full and frozen?"

"Yes," the voice confirmed.

"I'm confused," our cat said. "How do you put those two things together? You're keeping me alive *and* bringing me death?"

"Yes," the voice agreed. "It is confusing."

Our cat jumped in the air like she was poked by a stick. When she landed, she slowly walked toward a giant ant hill.

"Listen," the voice said. "This is important for you to understand. *You* are the leader. *You* are the one putting those thoughts together. *You* are the one making the decisions."

"I am confusing *you*?" she asked.

"Yes," the voice confirmed. "You are thinking like Nancy. Nancy is a confusing cat. She never knows what she wants. Good thoughts, bad thoughts, they are all random with Nancy. It means her voice is confused, too.

Once in a while something good might come her way, but usually bad things dominate her life. Her thought habit is lack and scarcity. Remember? Is that what you want?"

Thoughts of Nancy stirred up our cat's feelings of envy. "How come Big Jim doesn't have to worry about Frosty Time?" she pouted. "Why does he get to live with the people where it's warm? Why does he get everything while I get nothing?"

"You are thinking like Nancy again," the voice said. "When you are filled with envy, when you complain about what someone else has, your thought is still lack and scarcity."

After a long pause, our cat conceded, "I always think about Big Jim, plus being frozen…full of food…I think about that, too. A lot! How do I get these bad thoughts out of my head?"

"I have the answers for all of your questions," the voice said confidently.

Our cat sat down next to the dormant ant hill.

"While you are awake," the voice said, "you can only think one thought at a time. It will be either a good thought or a bad thought. It is impossible to think of both kinds of thoughts at the same time."

"The thought of me being frozen and full of food is a bad thought," she said.

"Yes," the voice agreed. "Now…look at the ant hill next to you. When it is warm, it is filled with tens of thousands of ants. That is about how many thoughts you have every day, and because there are so many, it is impossible for *you* to keep track of the good ones or the bad ones. The only way to tell is by knowing how you feel. Can you answer the questions? How do you feel?"

"I don't feel good," our cat conceded.

"You feel good?" asked the voice.

Our cat caught herself using the "don't" word. "I feel bad," she said sadly. "Bad."

"That explains it," the voice said. "When you have more bad thoughts versus good thoughts, you will feel bad. But if you can reverse it, have more good thoughts versus bad thoughts, you will *feel* good. When you feel good, I bring you good things."

"When I feel bad, you bring me bad things?" she asked.

"Yes," the voice agreed.

Good vibrations.

As the sun was warming the food field, the frost was melting, and the heat was rising, but our cat didn't notice. She was immersed, trying to figure out something important about her survival.

"It is all about your feelings," the voice continued. "Every thought has a vibration, like wings on a buzzing bee. Good thoughts bring good vibrations. Get enough of those, you feel good. Can you think of a good thought?"

"That's easy," our cat said. "It's when I entered the food field for the first time and found food. Every time I think about it I feel good."

"Yes," the voice said, "I agree. From now on, that will be your feel good thought."

"Feel good thought?" she asked.

"Yes," the voice said. "So…whenever you catch yourself feeling bad, you can block it by remembering your feel good thought."

"Like when I'm thinking about Big Jim," she confirmed.

"Yes," the voice agreed, "you can block it and stop it."

"Or when I think about being full and frozen," our cat continued.

"Yes," the voice said. "You block a bad thought with your feel good thought. Having the habit of using your feel good thought gives you the power to control your thoughts. The more you have good thoughts, the more you feel good."

"What I think about is what you bring about," she repeated.

"Yes," the voice agreed.

"When I think about food," she said, "you bring me food."

"Yes," the voice agreed, "because you believe in me I bring you food."

"What about the cold," our cat asked. "Do you bring me the cold?"

"Yes," the voice agreed. "You think about the cold a lot."

In the same way she thought about hunger, but really wanted food, our cat always thinks about how cold it is instead of imagining warmth.

"Whatever you think about the most is what I bring into your life," the voice said. "That means *you* are responsible for everything happening in your life right now, the food, the cold, the rat, staying away from people, living in a storm drain...all are the things you think about."

Our cat immediately became dejected. "What you're saying is all these things are the way they are now because of the way I think?"

"Yes," the voice confirmed.

"It's my fault I live in a storm drain?" she asked meekly.

"Yes," the voice confirmed again. "You have attracted all of these things into your life."

The idea began to sink in. She dropped her head, slouched her shoulders, then slowly walked back to her storm drain. As she took her seat on her perch, she fixed her eyes on the food field and began reflecting on how *she* was responsible for everything happening to her. It felt like there was no hope. Then...something magnificent happened! Instead of feeling sorry for herself, worrying about Frosty Time or being envious of Big Jim, she remembered her feel good thought.

"I feel good!" she cheered. "The sun is going down, I live in a storm drain, it's getting cold...and I feel good!"

Excitement began to build. She realized having the power to control her thoughts so she can think good thoughts versus bad thoughts means she has the power to change her life forever.

"I feel like I just learned a secret," our cat said, "a secret to the homeless cats, hungry cats, and cats in a struggle. If they knew the secret, how what they think about is what they bring about, they would have a better life; a life filled with abundance, like the abundance of food in the food field, a warm place to live, a place like...like...Big Jim's...a place...a home...with people."

"Yes," the voice said.

"And a name," she blurted out.

"Yes," the voice said.

If our cat had a name, it would come from the people, but she is afraid of them. How is that possible?

"I want a name," she declared.

"Names come from people," the voice warned. "People give you a name."

"I know," she replied. Our cat was not going to be defeated. She continued to think her feel good thought.

"When you *believe* in something like having a name," the voice said, "when you *believe* you *have* a name, I immediately start working on it for you because your wish is my command."

When she heard that, our cat was somewhat stumped. "How do I believe I have something when I don't know how it's going to happen?" our cat asked.

"Are you thinking like Nancy again?" the voice asked.

"Oh…wait…" she thought, "I get it…the how part. I don't need to know how it will happen. I need to believe it will happen."

"You need to believe it has _already_ happened," the voice said. "You need to expect it."

"How?" she asked. "How do I believe it has already happened?"

 "I have the answers for all of your questions," the voice said.

"We will change your lullaby to create *faith*…faith in you and me; faith in our ability to work together…to team up!"

It was very late. Our cat was ending a day when she learned so many big things. She got sleepy.

"Here is your new lullaby," the voice said. "I am so grateful and thankful for the abundance of food in the food field, and so grateful and thankful I have a name."

As our cat stood up and curled herself into a tight warm ball, the voice said "One more thing. As you say you are so grateful and thankful you have a name, I want you to imagine, visualize, and _remember_…people already giving you a name."

She closed her eyes, and began to repeat her new lullaby.

"I am so grateful and so thankful for the abundance of food in the food field, and so grateful and thankful I *have* a name. I am so grateful and so thankful for the abundance of food in the food field, and so grateful and thankful I *have* a name. I am so grateful and so thankful for the abundance of food in the food field, and so grateful and thankful I *have* a name. I am so grateful and so thankful for the abundance of food in the food field, and so grateful and thankful I *have* a name. I am so grateful and so thankful for the abundance of food in the food field, and so grateful and thankful I *have* a name. I am so grateful...purr...purr...purr."

Strategy 8

Always feel good.

Imagine tens of thousands of thoughts going through your head every day. The only way to know you're thinking more good thoughts than bad thoughts is knowing how you feel. If you feel good, you are thinking more good thoughts rather than bad ones. If you feel bad, you know what that means.

If you're breaking even, where some are good and some are bad, you are confusing your subconscious mind.

Unfortunately, this happens for most cats like Negative Nancy.

For cats who feel bad all the time, creating good vibrations, feeling good, is really hard! The best way to make it happen is block those bad thoughts with a feel good thought. Do it enough times on purpose and your bad thoughts will soon vanish.

Strategy 9

Create faith.

When you repeat something to yourself over and over again, and you believe it's already happened (and "remembering" it makes it even more powerful), you are creating faith. When you have faith, you have the power to attract the things you want in your life.

Do this at the end of your day and the beginning of the next day for at least four to six weeks.

Visualizing what you want is important, too. Visualizing what you want and combining it with emotions makes the message very clear to your subconscious mind.

Repetition and expectancy create faith.

Strategy 10

Wish the best for everyone.

Feelings of envy mean bad thoughts and bad feelings for <u>you</u>. When you think bad thoughts about someone else, they end up creating a "boomerang" that comes back to you. Let it go! Wish the best for those who already enjoy life filled with abundance. When you do, you attract good things into your life too!

Chapter 5: Desire Your Dream

If repetition with emotional visualization are keys to fast and effective communication to her subconscious mind (her voice), our cat already has a name even though she doesn't know it yet! It is part of her lullaby, she is constantly repeating "I have a name" to herself, plus she can close her eyes anytime and visualize a person standing in front of her giving her a name. She could easily be discouraged because it's hard to believe in something that has not happened yet, but armed with her feel good thought, nothing will stop her from attracting the people, place, or moment.

How?

Frosty Time could make a rude entrance into her life any day, but she's not worried. Instead, she sits on her perch in the storm drain, deep in thought, staring at the tall house across the street just a little bit up the hill. Even though she's afraid of people, she's imagining living in it, getting food when she wants while staying warm during Frosty Time. Every once in a while you can hear what sounds like crying, "MEEOOOWWW," but it's really cat lingo for *how*. How will she get in the tall house? How will she get the people to give her a name? Even more important, how can she become a part of their family?

The vibration from the meowing was so loud it shook the rat out of his slumber.

"Wut's this here-a racket all about," shouted the slow talking rat. Then he realized who it was. "Oh…my gosh…it's you kitten…er I mean…uh…cat."

"I have a name," our cat angrily declared.

"Oh you dooooo," the rat replied. "Ya have a name? I'm so very, very, very, happy for ya. What, pray tell, is ya name? That a way I'll be shore next time we chat I won't be so insensitive."

"I don't know my name yet," she snapped. "I just know I have one."

"That's a little bit confusin'," the rat replied to the echo of his buddies giggling in the background. "Ya don't know what your name is yet, but ya know ya got one. How come?"

The rat has no idea about the transformation in our cat's life, doesn't know about the voice, how she's been devouring so many of his little friends in the food field, or how committed she is to having a name.

"Go away, rat," she said. "I'm not answering your question. I have a name. That's final!"

"Of course," the rat replied sympathetically. "No one's questionin' your character here-a. When ya do know what your name is, why we ought to have a celebration. I know all my friends here would like to come. Wouldn't ya boys?"

The sound of the squealing rats reached a crescendo, but soon faded as they slowly waddled back into the sewer.

Make a decision.

"I hear you," the voice said. "I hear what you are thinking, I see what you are thinking, and I am sensing your dream. What it feels like is another miracle is on its way to you."

Our cat has already received one miracle, but this one feels complicated to her. People are involved. She knows she needs people for what she wants, but she's still afraid of them.

"You have a strong faith for having a name," the voice observed. "Ignoring the rat's suggestion proves it."

"How will I get the people to let me live in their house and be a part of their family?" she asked.

 "I have the answers for all of your questions," the voice said.

She waited for what seemed like a long time, but after a while, it became clear to her that an answer was not forthcoming, at least not right now. "Okay," she said almost impatiently, "what is the answer?"

"You are right," the voice confirmed. "This will be different from a healing."

It felt like the voice was preparing her for a bleak outcome. In that moment, she forgot her feel good thought. Her shoulders slumped.

"Cats like Nancy make a mistake," the voice said. "They think they must know how a miracle is going to happen before it can happen. The reality is miracles are impossible to explain. That's why they're called miracles."

"I want a miracle," our cat pleaded. "I want to live with the people where it is warm, and they give me food. I want it with all my heart."

"You have a dream," the voice observed, "a dream so powerful it is filling you with desire, so much desire a miracle *is* possible."

As she heard the encouragement, positive feelings flooded her mind lead by her feel good thought. Positive ideas have a way of blocking negative ideas every time.

"It is time to make a decision," the voice said. "It is time to decide what you want, your heart's desire, your dream."

Our cat was trying to understand.

After a long pause, the voice continued. "A decision is what you make when you declare your desire…your dream. You tell the cat universe what you want. It is you saying 'what I want is what I'm going to get.' It is you saying, 'I am going to do everything I can to make it happen until it happens.' It is you saying, 'here we go' and 'I am going to keep moving my paws until what I want to have happen…happens!' It is the kind of dream that means you forget wishing, forget hoping, and forget quitting. It is a commitment without compromise."

"The how part," our cat said, "is what Nancy would be demanding to know."

"Yes," the voice said. "Yet the first and most important thing to do after you know *what* your dream is and after you discover your dream, is to make the decision to get it. Only then will the *how* part be revealed to us. So what is your dream? What do you want?"

Without any hesitation, she declared, "I want the people to give me a name."

"You already have a name," the voice promptly insisted.

"What is it?" she demanded.

"Patience," the voice cautioned. "These things take time."

"How much time?" she pressed. "When will I know?"

"When a seed finds its way underground," the voice said, "you can't see it, but something is happening. It's growing. The same is true for your name. Something has already started, something is happening. Continuing your lullaby, repeating your dream, those things help, but hear this; your faith in me means it has already happened. There is no need to ask for it again. Simply expect it."

Our cat decided the voice was right. She already has a name, but she still wants more. She stood up from her perch, did a 360 then sat back down to stare at the tall house across the street.

"You have the opportunity to live a joyous and abundant life, filled with love and beauty," the voice said. "I can fulfill your every wish when we agree on what you want. Then we can team up to make it happen"

"I don't want to live in this storm drain anymore," she declared. She forgot about the "don't" word again.

"Your dream is to live in this storm drain?" the voice asked quizzically.

She panicked. "I DON'T WANT TO LIVE IN THE STORM DRAIN!"

The voice was being patient. "Ask me again," the voice encouraged. "Ask for what you truly dream about…for what you truly want. Ask so I'll understand exactly what you want and there is absolutely no confusion."

She started remembering what she learned in the food field, how she was responsible for attracting everything in her life, and how she realized she has the power to control her thoughts, giving her the power to change her life forever.

"Okay" she finally blurted. "I know what I really want…I know what my dream is…but I'm afraid if I ask for it, I won't get it…that I'll fail. I want to live in the tall house with the people, but I'm afraid of them. I'm *really* afraid of people."

The voice reassured her. "That is what is so fantastic about this whole thing. When you overcome your fear of people, you will be in the position to receive your dream! You could make some mistakes along the way. You may even fail trying, but your desire and perseverance will give you the strength you need. Now…what is your *dream*?"

She couldn't hold back any longer. She's been imagining it for days, and now she's saying it out loud:

"I want to live with the people in the tall house," she roared, "and I want a door with my name on it! A door I can go in when I'm hungry; a door I can go in when Frosty Time comes."

As our cat was declaring her decision, her tail started to vibrate with great energy. A huge gust of wind began to blow in the night. Fall leaves swirled inside the storm drain cavern, surrounding her like with whirlwind. When she finished her thought the wind died, dropping the leaves to the floor. Then…there in radiant beauty, glowing in the dark was our cat, chest out, back straight, eyes wide open, tail thumping the edge of her perch.

Our cat had discovered her purpose!

"Yes," the voice confirmed. "Now you know what your dream is and you've said it out loud. You want to live with the people in the tall house. It is your purpose."

By knowing her purpose, she has a chance to live, because Frosty Time can swiftly end it.

"When," the voice asked, "when do you want it to happen?"

With great confidence, she replied, "I want to live with the people in the tall house before Frosty Time comes."

Then the voice asked, "What are you willing to give in exchange for this?"

She was stumped. "What do you mean, give?" she asked. "I have nothing to give."

"But you do," the voice proffered. "You have something very powerful to give. In exchange for living with the people...YOU will give them *love*."

"Love?" she asked. "What's love?"

Love is something a homeless feral cat lacks. It goes back to their parents, always anxious to wean their kittens. There was never enough time to teach love and affection. No wonder our cat doesn't know what love is.

"Love is difficult to explain," the voice said, "especially to a cat who has never loved before. So...for now, love means you let the people pet you."

"What does that mean?" she asked.

"People will stroke you and rub you and scratch you with their fingertips," the voice said.

"YIKES!" she exclaimed.

"Remember closing your eyes and turning your shoulder into Big Jim?" the voice asked. "What cats do just before they rub another cat? It's one of the first signs you love someone. When you do that with people, they will pet you, they will love you then you will love them."

"So I let the people pet me?" she asked.

"Yes," the voice said.

"Will they hurt me?" she asked.

"When you start curling and purring around their legs, they will not move," the voice said. "They may use their fingers to rub your back then scratch your ears. It will feel good."

Wanting to be reassured, she asked "You are sure they will be nice to me?"

"Yes," the voice confirmed. "But they will be more worried about you being nice to them. It's why you curl and purr around their legs. It lets them learn to trust you."

Our cat and the voice kept talking into the night until they finally agreed on a new lullaby:

"I am so grateful and thankful for the abundance of food in the food field, I am so grateful and thankful I have a name, and I am so grateful and thankful I am living with the people in the tall house before Frosty Time comes, and in return I will give them love."

Strategy 11

Make a decision.

Too often cats fail to make a decision to fulfill a dream because they don't know how it will happen. Failing to make a decision means you get less.

But when you have the habit of deciding what you want then have faith in your subconscious mind's ability to manifest your dream into your physical life, that's where it gets exciting.

The "how" part comes AFTER you make your decision.

The voice asked our cat to make her decision even stronger by encouraging her to commit to *when* she was going to live with the people and what she would *give* in return.

When you make a decision, it creates a wave, a vibration, an energy. The bigger your decision, the bigger your vibration is.

A Special Bonus from Bill

I am so thankful and grateful you have a copy of Strategies for Cats! It is my sincere hope that, by reading this book, you change the way you think so you can receive the abundance you deserve!

To express my gratitude, I'd like to give you a free, beautiful PDF featuring the 22 Strategies for Cats. It's a convenient and easy way to review and remember all the Strategies, and perfect for your refrigerator door!

To receive your free copy of the 22 Strategies for Cats suitable for framing, please visit our website:

http://www.strategiesforcats.com/bookbonus

To contact me for speaking engagements on Strategies for Cats, visit:

http://www.billajohnston.com

Plus, for even more on the book, the adventures of Kitty, and me, visit and like our Facebook page:

http://www.facebook.com/strategiesforcats

Chapter 6: Take Action

Three days have passed since our cat put her huge thought into the universe...a thought so big it's become her purpose. No longer is she obsessed with what she wants; she knows what it is. She has declared it. The *how* part, *that* is still unknown.

She shouldn't have any worries though. The voice has consistently explained it has all the answers for her questions, so she is confident it will help her with the *how* part. Only one problem: The voice has mysteriously gone silent.

Our cat puts herself in the position to hear her voice. She sits on her perch for long periods of time, staring at the tall house she wants to live in, wanders the food field even when she's not hungry, hoping somewhere around the big ant hill the voice would return with some wisdom, some companionship, even at night when it seems easier to talk to the voice or in the morning as she wakes up, she is asking...waiting.

The voice is not speaking.

The good news is she is clinging to her lullaby and repeating her purpose so often it has become an obsession. Sometimes she even puts herself into a sleepy trance.

The nudge.

Sitting on her perch, staring at the tall house, our cat watched the sun go down, then the full moon come up. As she imagined living inside, she named it her "Dream Home."

After some time, she decided to crawl out of her storm drain and walk up the hill toward Jim's house. While she did, she enjoyed looking at her Dream Home. She can see the driveway, the zoomway door, and the back yard. As she stopped to stare, she began repeating her purpose.

"I am so grateful and thankful I am living with the people in my Dream Home before Frosty Time comes, and in return I will give them love." She was so emotional she was almost in tears.

Then, out of nowhere, she got an idea! It came like a nudge; the same kind of nudge she felt when the voice warned her about danger. She couldn't put the nudge into words, couldn't hear exactly what it was saying, but she knew what it was saying. What excited her was she immediately knew it was the voice...*her* voice. It gave her an idea to move her paws, take action, and go to her Dream Home.

She bolted across the street, headed straight to the mouth of the zoomway, then suddenly stopped. She stared at her Dream Home for a moment then cautiously walked toward the zoomway door. As she got closer, her eyes got bigger. She was smiling! As she approached she remembered what Big Jim's door looked like, the door with his name on it.

"Jim's door was right here," she thought to herself as she touched a spot on the bottom of the huge zoomway door with her paw.

Ever so faintly, the voice said, "Yes," but she didn't hear it.

"He can put his paw on it just like this, and then it opens so he can go in it." As she removed her paw she left a paw-print, a paw-print right where she imagined her door would be.

"Look," she said enthusiastically, "here's *my* door!" She was admiring the paw print, proud of the moment, excited she was actually in front the of the zoomway door at her Dream Home.

"Yes," the voice said louder.

Her head perked up. She heard it. "Is that you?" she asked excitedly.

"Yes," the voice said.

"Where have you been?" she asked.

"I...am...you," the voice reminded her. "I am here. I have always been here. You can count on me. You can believe in me. You can..."

"Kachunk...chunk...chunk...chunk...chunk... chunk..."

Our cat did a quick body flip in mid-air then landed on all fours with the look of terror in her eyes. "What is that?" she exclaimed.

The zoomway door was making a huge noise. It was going up and up and up until it was gone! Walking around the zoom machine heading right toward her was one of the people. It was a man, a really tall man. Then...he saw her.

"Hey!" he yelled. "What are you doing here, cat? Get out of here! I don't want a cat in my life!"

Our cat seized back, did a 180, put her tail under legs, and blazed down the zoomway, across the street, down the hill then leaped into her storm drain.

"Whew!" she thought, gasping for air. "That was close!"

"Yes," the voice chided. "Your first encounter with one of the people you want to live with *was* close, so close something exciting *could* have happened."

The voice was helping our cat understand when you ask for something, the universe can transform thoughts into her material life quickly.

"But you heard what he said," she exclaimed, "He doesn't want a cat in his life."

"I heard him say he *wants* a cat in his life," the voice said. "That's what you want too."

As our cat was catching her breath, she remembered how her voice doesn't hear "don't." She picked her head up then started thumping her tail. The encouragement was working until she was startled by the of sound the tall man's voice right outside her storm drain. She was petrified!

"Here cat. Here kitty, kitty cat," the tall man was coaxing. "Come here kitty kitty…come here…"

The tall man was on one knee with an outstretched hand peering into our storm drain. She couldn't see his face. The moon was behind him, but he could easily see her big eyes glowing from the reflection.

"Come on kitty cat. Come on out here!" he said again.

Fear of people flooded our cat's mind. She kept perfectly still, thinking he couldn't see her or would forget about her then go away.

Losing interest, he stood, turned then walked up the hill, across the street, into the zoomway toward her Dream Home. As he did, our cat took action again! She followed him across the street then up the zoomway!

Just as the tall man got to the house he turned to look toward the storm drain only to be surprised by who was following him. He walked back toward her. "Hey!" he said warmly. "Here cat. Here kitty cat. Come here…COME HERE!"

"WWWWAAAA!" she screeched, did another 180 then retreated to safety again.

With all the lullabies, the staring, the dreaming, one would think she should have been ready to receive her miracle, but some cats tell themselves big things take time. The reality is they don't. The universe likes speed.

The frustrated tall man turned to his house. As the zoomway door was closing behind him, you could hear him mumbling, "Why is it whenever you want to pet a cat, it has to be their idea?"

As the zoomway door closed a light behind it evaporated. Then, after watching every light inside her Dream Home go away, she reemerged from her storm drain, sat on the brown round thing for a long time then crossed the street like a thief in the night. She stopped at the bottom of the zoomway to make sure the coast was clear, then quickly walked back to the zoomway door, cutting eyes in all directions, making sure she was not being watched.

When she arrived at the zoomway door…HER door…she did a couple of slow 360s then let out a big sigh while sitting in front of it like she was home. Our cat was so grateful and so thankful to be next to her door at her Dream Home she laid down…closed her eyes…THEN FELL FAST ASLEEP!

After nighttime passed and the sun came out she was still there! She slept on the zoomway all night! And then.

"Kachunk…chunk…chunk…chunk…chunk…
chunk…"

"OH MY GOSH!" she thought.

"WAKE UP" the voice yelled, "WAKE UP!"

The zoomway door was opening! The tall man was
getting in his zoom machine!

VAROOM! "The zoom machine is going!!!" she said.
"The zoom machine is going!!!"

Our cat's frightened look and back flip was a sight to
behold! She fell on her hips, jumped up in the air then
bolted for her storm drain. But when the zoom machine
slowly rolled into the street, it kept going backward until it
stopped in front of the storm drain. Then, the window
rolled down and the tall man stuck his head out. "Are you
in there kitty cat?" he asked. "Kitty cat…HEY!!" As he
turned his head in disappointment, the window went up,
the zoom machine roared up the street then the tall man
was gone.

As the noise faded from the storm drain, our cat was
left staring intently at her Dream Home, and even though
she was shivering and shaking, <u>her desire to achieve her
purpose was not shaken</u>.

Ideas.

The voice gave her time to calm down. It could have
criticized her for not seeing her opportunity to achieve her

purpose, but the voice is patient. Instead, the voice will focus on the positive, say good things about what she did right, and encourage her to believe in herself.

"You did something that was very good," the voice said.

Our cat raised and tilted her head like she was hearing a beautiful song.

"You were courageous," the voice said. "It took courage to go to the zoomway door the first time; courage to follow the tall man back to your Dream Home." The voice knew she would need courage to survive the quickly approaching Frosty Time.

She straightened her back and expanded her chest with pride. The thought of fleeing, being a coward, fearing the people, never came forward. "Where did you go?" she asked. "I thought I lost you."

"I…am…you," the voice said again. "I have always been here, and I will always be here. I am here when you are awake; I am here when you sleep. You can always count on me."

"I couldn't hear you," she confessed. "I had questions to ask you." Then, as if a title wave of thought went through her mind, she got it. "YOU…YOU told me to go the zoomway door," she exclaimed.

"You have the answers to all my questions," she continued.

"Yes," the voice said. "I…am…the *creative* you. When you ask questions, when you are curious, when you need an idea, I am the creative you. I provide you with answers from me and from the universe."

The voice continued. "The amazing power you just learned is that you know I am here. You already know how to ask me questions, now you understand how to listen for my answers. Yes, that was me on the hill giving you the nudge, the idea, the answer to your questions; how to start pursuing your purpose. You heard me, and then you took action."

Our cat was excited to hear she was on the right path, proud she was doing the right things, but she felt she was about to lose the only friend she has. "What's going to happen when I can't hear you?" she asked.

"I will always be here," the voice replied, "but your gift…of hearing my voice…that is going away soon. You can tell."

Strategy 12

Take action.

When you make a decision, when you know your purpose, it can be very exciting when you use the Law of Attraction to attract what you want into your material life. But you can't be stuck on a perch or a couch. You'll need to get up and do something. Take action, even if it is wrong.

Strategy 13

Focus on the positive.

It is easy to focus on what someone is doing wrong. That's how you get more wrong stuff! When the voice focused on what our cat was doing right — being courageous — the voice will get more of the good stuff, in this case, courage.

People who know how to do this get more out of themselves and others.

Chapter 7: Try Again

Fear of failure has the power to stop some cats from achieving their goals and dreams. Maybe that's why when cats like Negative Nancy make a first attempt at achieving something and it ends poorly, their thought habit, their negative thoughts of lack and scarcity, dominate their thinking. So they forget about it.

Success, achievements, and positive things each need to be thought about on purpose for our cat. It's this new habit that has given her the power to make negative thoughts go away. When she thinks her feel good thought, she feels good and returns to positive thinking to achieve her purpose.

That's the range of emotions our cat has gone through after reliving her adventure with the tall man. Now she's feeding her voice with images, visualizing living in her Dream Home, and living with the people. As a result, her voice must manifest her purpose into her material life the fastest and most expedient way possible.

Try again.

It's nighttime. Our cat is sitting on the brown round thing, staring at her Dream Home, repeating her purpose. She can see her breath. It's cold. "I am so grateful and thankful I am living with the people in my Dream Home before Frosty Time comes, and in return I will give them love." She is very committed, yet still fearful of people. But she knows she has to overcome it, and she will. She is creating faith in herself.

"I can see what you are thinking," the voice said. "You can see your Dream Home, the tall man, and your door. You are repeating those things over and over. There *is* more."

"I know," she replied. "There are more people inside. I am still afraid of the people. How will I get them to like me? How will I get them to love me?"

"You have the answers to all my questions," she continued.

"It is natural to be afraid of the unknown, but when you learn what you are afraid of, the same courage you showed going to the zoomway door, following the man ...that kind of courage will make your fear of people...flee!"

Our cat is sitting proudly, tail straight up in the air, head cocked, looking very confident. "I am a courageous cat," she declared.

"Yes," the voice agreed. "You are a courageous cat, a courageous cat who knows what she wants. Now…as you imagine living with the people in your Dream Home, giving them love, what do you see?"

"I want to see inside," she said. "I want to see the people living inside."

"Yes," the voice agreed.

The voice didn't say the words. It gave our cat a nudge to *try again*. She raced to the bottom of the zoomway. The moon was glowing. She could see her shadow. Slowly, she walked to the zoomway door, stopped to stare at her paw print, closed her eyes then imagined her door being there. She started bobbing her head up and down as if she was about to get sleepy. She was concentrating on this being *her* door, *her* Dream Home, and she was *feeling* good.

Our cat was so entranced she lost her balance then fell sideways on the zoomway. "Meow!" she exclaimed. She quickly jumped to her feet, looked to see if she was being watched, then cautiously crept toward the back of her Dream Home. There she saw windows with small ledges on them.

The first window was dark, but the second was bright and inviting. She carefully coiled herself, got her footing right then jumped on the ledge.

"Look!" she thought, "there are 1…2…3…4 people, they're talking loud, there's a green tree, and what's those sing-song sounds? The people are putting round things on the green tree. I've never seen a tree like that before."

What surprised her more than the sights and sounds was the warmth coming from the window. "Oh, it's so warm, and I'm so cold," she thought. Then something came over her. She closed her eyes, dipped her shoulder then began rocking her body against the window. Back and forth, back and forth, every time she got a little warmer on one side of her body, so warm she thought she could do it to her other side. So she jumped off the ledge, jumped to her other side then thought "Oh…oh…I'm so happy."

Our cat was rubbing the window over and over. It was as if she putting herself in a daze, when suddenly the good feelings came to an abrupt end.

TAP TAP TAP!

A sound she could hear AND feel. She opened her eyes with a say-what look on her face. Behind the window was one of the people, not the tallest one; it was a smaller one with long black hair named Jennifer. Her face was pressed into the glass. "Look Mom, a cat!" she shouted, the sound muffled by the window.

Our cat was so frightened she pushed off the ledge doing a 360 in the midair then fell to the big wood floor on her hip with a thud.

"MEOW!"

She couldn't move her paws fast enough. She fled, ran down the zoomway then disappeared in the storm drain.

Jennifer ran out the door, chasing her down the zoomway. "Here cat! Here kitty cat!" she yelled.

Big lights turned on while her tall Mom with long red hair followed Jennifer outside.

"Mom," Jennifer said, "it's so cold out here, and that poor little cat's out here all alone!"

"How do you know?" Mom asked. "She probably belongs to one of the neighbors."

"Maaaaam! I've never seen her before," Jennifer insisted. "I'm gonna give her some milk." As she went in the house, her Mom strolled down the zoomway closer to the street. When Jennifer returned she was carefully carrying a bowl of milk. Surprisingly she placed it in front of our cat's paw print on the zoomway door.

"Here cat. Here kitty cat!" Jennifer yelled. With the crisp night air, her voice carried across the street, filling the storm drain with the sweetest sound of calling. Then Jennifer walked to the bottom of the zoomway while staring at the storm drain. "Come on cat. Here cat, here kitty cat," she begged.

Jennifer tried to tip toe into the street, but Mom caught her. "Jennifer, don't go over there. Get back inside." Mom was standing at the top of the zoomway, hands on hips, with a big light behind her. You could only see her shadow and breath from the cold air. "It's too late to be out here all by yourself!" Reluctantly, Jennifer quickly stood, pouted, clenched her fists then briskly walked straight armed up the zoomway. Soon, the big light went away. The excitement was over…for the moment.

As our cat crouched down on her perch, she noticed something in the air, an aroma she normally doesn't smell. She jumped on top of the brown round thing then scooted back across the street. The smell was coming from the front of the zoomway door…her door! Without hesitation, she ran to the milk.

"WOW," she thought. "It's delicious!"

Licking as fast as she could, she drained the bowl clean, then in the excitement knocked it upside down.

CLANG!

That scared her! She scooted down the zoomway and leaped into her storm drain, but this time with a tummy full of milk. She forgot about the cold, the fear, instead she was fulfilled…feeling fantastic.

Gratitude.

Sleep was hard to come by after the excitement of going to her Dream Home, seeing Jennifer face to face, and the milk. She loves the milk. "I want more," she said. "It was so good, so delicious, how do I get more?"

The voice could feel her excitement. At a time of day when homeless cats are cold and hungry, our cat was enthused, alive, and optimistic. "Gratitude," the voice advised. "Thank Big Cat for these blessings. When you are thankful, when you express true gratitude, you get more."

Our cat closed her eyes to pray to Big Cat just like the voice taught her. She said, "Big Cat, WOW, thank you for giving me my purpose, for letting me live in my Dream Home, and for the people. I love the people, and am thankful they are a part of my life. Big Cat, I am also *very* grateful and thankful for the milk. Yes, I am grateful and thankful for the abundance of food in the food field, but now I am even more grateful and thankful for milk from Jennifer. Thank you Big Cat, thank you."

Strategy 14

Try again.

Failure happens all the time. Don't be discouraged. Be encouraged. It's in the past. The past has no bearing on what the future holds for you.

Sometimes the biggest gain you'll ever make will be after the biggest failure you have ever had.

When you are filled with desire, when you have a sense of purpose, you know your purpose, and you are determined, your dream will come true.

So don't stop. Keep going. Try again.

Strategy 15

Positive prayer.

When you pray, it is the only time you can communicate directly to your subconscious mind, Big Cat and the universe, so it is an extremely powerful way to convey your desires and your dreams.

Too often prayer is a tool of "last resort," where there may be desperation, pain, or real suffering. Unfortunately for cats who pray with those negative thoughts, they may be asking for relief, asking for help, asking for a miracle, but those are not the prevailing thoughts on their mind. They're usually dwelling on the negative things, the negative thoughts, and because "your wish is my command," a negative prayer will have negative results.

When you pray for positive things with positive feelings, pray with emotion, pray in the present tense as if you have already received them, then you attract more good feelings, good thoughts, and good things into your life.

Chapter 8: Perseverance

After a cold night, our cat wakes up remembering how it ended, because even though she was still afraid of the people, the milk was magnificent. She saw inside the tall home, the place where she wants to live, and began imagining what it would be like.

"When I live in the tall house with the people, I hope they give me milk all the time," she said. "I wonder if Big Jim gets milk all the time, too." She crawled out of her storm drain then sat on the brown round thing to stare at her Dream Home. When she looked up the hill she saw Big Jim looking down at her. Feelings of envy flooded her thoughts.

"I hate Big Jim," our cat said bluntly. She angrily stared back.

"I know Big Jim has caused you pain," the voice said. "But think about your feelings. Are you feeling good, or are you feeling bad?"

Without hesitation, she replied, "I'm feeling bad."

"Yes," the voice agreed. "Your emotion is envy, and even though you have done nothing wrong, envy always makes *you* feel bad."

Our cat couldn't listen to her voice, didn't care about good feelings versus bad feelings. The bitterness and angst took over her emotions.

"What you think about is what I bring about," the voice reminded her. The voice controls our cat's emotions. She continued to fume.

"Envy has the power to defeat your miracle," the voice said.

That got our cat's attention. She stood, shook herself from head to tail. Finally, she looked away from Big Jim to turn her attention toward her Dream Home. A positive idea can defeat a negative one every time.

"Repeat your purpose," the voice encouraged.

Sitting back down she said, "I am so grateful and thankful I am living with the people in my Dream Home before Frosty Time comes, and in return I will give them love."

The voice was leading our cat toward the power of forgiveness, helping her to understand it is impossible to love one and hate another at the same time. She wasn't ready.

"I can't think about this," our cat insisted. She jumped off the brown round thing then headed to the food field. First she trotted then ran as if she was fleeing Jim, remembering how he hurt her, how she still resents *he* is the one enjoying a life filled with abundance, while she is settling for mice.

But as our cat crept into the food field, she heard an unusual noise from deep inside the tall grass, a noise she had never heard before. It was mice…a lot of them…squealing and squeaking around something lying on the ground behind a bush. They were eating it!

Our cat crouched down and slowly crept toward the noise, slipping through tall blades of grass and weeds until she got close enough to make out something, only to be surprised by a familiar voice.

"Oh…uh…hello kitten…I mean… um… cat… uh… whatever your name is. Why…what brings you down here-a?"

IT WAS THE RAT! Our cat had never seen the rat in the food field. He was trailed by three other rats, all of them shiny black with snarly little faces. Then it occurred to her she's living with all of them in her storm drain. Ugh!

"What are you doing here rat?" our cat asked firmly.

"Well, an unfortunate series of events occurred yesterday," the rat said, "and…uh…well as a result of some food fallin' from the sky, we was just eatin' all we could before all them mice showed up and shoved us out of the way."

Then something came over the rat. It was like he was salivating over our cat like SHE was food.

"What's in there?" she demanded.

The rat ignored her question, instead opened his mouth to reveal some impressive teeth. Then…he tried to take a bite out of her!

WACK, WACK, WACK, WACK!

Four quick smacks across the rat's face were all it took from our cat to roll him over a few times.

When he returned to his feet, the rat said, "We all not hungry right now *kitten*, but next time you take a swipe at me, you best be ready, 'cause we ALL won't stop 'til you're just like your friend back there-a!"

As the rats waddled away with their newly fattened bodies, our cat turned her attention back to the noise. As she crept closer, she could see the image of a face, a face she recognized, a face lying sideways on the ground. Its head was moving a little bit but its eyes weren't. When she got closer…she realized…

THAT'S NANCY! NANCY THE CAT IS BEHIND THAT BUSH, AND SHE'S BEING EATEN BY THE MICE!

NANCY THE CAT HAS BEEN KILLED!

She did the fastest 180 ever, running like a crazy cat to…wait a minute! Going to the storm drain means being with the rat who just tried to bite her. She screeched to a halt, thought for a moment then reluctantly slipped onto her perch. She had to hide somewhere.

While catching her breath, it all started to sink in. "They killed Nancy!" she blurted. "She's dead!"

"MEEEEEEOOOOOWWWWW...MEEEEEEOOOOOOWWW! Oh...MEEEEEEOOOOWWWWW..."

Our cat cried and cried. She dropped her head to her paws, started shivering and shaking, but couldn't close her eyes. She couldn't get the image out of her mind. Fear was creeping back in. "How did they kill Nancy? Did the rat kill Nancy? Are the mice so mad at cats they've ganged up and are now killing us? Was Nancy their first cat? If they could kill Nancy, could they kill me? What if I stay in this storm drain? Will I die during Frosty Time? Or if I try to wait it out and live through the Frosty Time, will the rats eat me in my sleep?"

Our cat was panicking.

"What you think about is what I bring about," the voice said. The voice controls our cat's emotions. Now she is filled with panic and fear.

Then, another reality set in.

"How can I go back to the food field," she whimpered. "How can I face seeing Nancy like that? What am I going to do?"

"Nancy was a part of a family," the voice counseled. "The people will find her and put her in the ground."

"Why did Nancy get killed?" she asked.

"Nancy's thought habit was negative," the voice said. "That means she attracted negative things into her life."

"So was Nancy thinking about death?" she asked.

"She was in the wrong place at the wrong time," the voice said. "Big birds looking for opportunity, big birds thinking about food, they were attracted to her. After they found her and killed her, they received their food. It's the same thing you do in the food field."

"If I think negative thoughts, negative things will happen to me?" she asked.

"Yes," the voice confirmed.

"If I think positive thoughts, if I think abundance, positive things will happen to me?" she asked.

"Yes," the voice confirmed again.

Perseverance.

It was quiet in the storm drain. Our cat was thinking about how hard her life was, how Big Jim attacked her and almost killed her, how the rats would like to eat her, how she eats the mice, and now how the big birds ate Nancy."

"You are thinking about the circle of life," the voice said. "Everyone needs food to eat, unfortunately where you are in life, where you have decided to live, you could be a part of it, too."

The voice was giving her time to think, time to catch her feel good thought, time to remember her purpose.

"Big Cat has already lined up a new path for you," the voice said. "When you declared your purpose, I felt what

Big Cat did for you. Now it is time to claim the life you want, believe in the joy waiting for you. You have shown yourself to be a cat of courage, a cat of perseverance, a cat of faith, and a cat who will never give up. The two of us, you and me working as a team, can accomplish your dream and live a life of harmony with the people in your Dream Home."

"I am a cat of courage," she proclaimed.

"Yes," the voice said.

The day was so traumatic our cat got sleepy, so sleepy her mind cleared out…thinking of absolutely nothing. It was as if she was listening for a little voice…*her* voice. She closed her eyes, started to bob her head from side to side. Soon, she was fast asleep. When she woke her mind was alert, ready to ask questions.

"How will I get all the people to love me," she asked.

"I have the answers for all of your questions," the voice said.

Then, just like the nudge going to Jim's house, the nudge to go to the zoomway door, she felt another nudge…an idea.

"You're telling me to not worry about all four people," our cat said.

"Yes," the voice said.

"You're telling me to pick one," she said, "pick the easiest, pick Jennifer."

"Yes," the voice said.

Every day the big yellow zoom machine goes past the storm drain to the bottom of the zoomway to pick up Jennifer, and every day it drops Jennifer off.

"Let's move our paws," the voice encouraged. "The big yellow zoom machine should be here soon. That's when Jennifer will be at the bottom of the zoomway."

Our cat leaned forward on her perch as if she were ready to jump out.

"Put yourself in the position to make something happen," the voice said. "When Jennifer gets off the big yellow zoom machine, I want you be there, posing, so when she sees you, she will be attracted to you."

She coiled up then bolted out of the storm drain, across the street, up the hill then sat at the bottom of the zoomway.

"POSE!" the voice yelled. "Pose like your life depends on it!"

Our cat had her tail straight up in the air as she was sitting with her head slightly cocked…almost cracking a confident smile.

"You are so attractive," the voice encouraged, "you are so beautiful, you are so amazing! Now keep posing until Jennifer is here."

Soon the sound of the big yellow zoom machine could be heard in the distance. It got louder, turned the corner then rolled up the hill toward our cat. You could hear the sound of little people squealing, saying things like "look at the kitty." It was so loud it excited Jennifer because the kitty was at her house!

Strategy 16

Take something apart.

If a job or a task feels too big, break it into smaller pieces, and then take them on one at a time.

Instead of trying to love all four people, the voice gave our cat the idea to start with one…one at a time.

Strategy 17

Perseverance.

Don't stop. Don't ever surrender until your purpose is achieved.

Chapter 9: Love

As the big yellow zoom machine came to a loud stop, an opening door released the sound of excited little people cooing. It was so loud it startled our cat. She jumped up the in air.

"Stay," the voice said. "You are a courageous cat."

She stopped herself from fleeing to the storm drain. Instead our cat slow walked off the zoomway, found a spot on the grass, slowly twirled two times, then sat down with her tail straight up.

Jennifer carefully walked down the tall steps while little faces were peering out the door and windows, hoping to catch a glimpse of our cat. When the door squealed closed, the big yellow zoom machine made a thunderous sound as it pulled away, leaving an unpleasant plume of smoke. Jennifer eagerly dropped a bag from her back to the ground then slowly walked toward our cat.

"Aw…" Jennifer said quietly while looking directly into our cat's eyes. "You're the cat that lives in the storm drain over there. Aren't you kitty?"

She remembered Jennifer's face from the first time she saw it through the window. A good feeling was coming over her until her voice gave her some confusing advice.

"Look away," the voice said.

"Huh?" she thought.

"Yes," the voice said. "Look away. People petting you must be your idea."

Our cat dutifully looked away but couldn't help thumping her tail on the ground. Thump…thump… thump…the rhythm, the vibration, something is coming over her. She's getting excited because her purpose is happening before her little eyes.

"People want what they can't have," the voice said, "so stand up, then walk away."

Reluctantly our cat took the direction, but was immediately distracted by Jennifer.

"Where are you going kitty?" she squawked. "Come here. Come here and sniff my hand." Jennifer was bending down, elbows straddling her legs, hand outstretched toward our cat, moving her fingers like she was snapping them but making no sounds.

One step away, two steps away, three steps away, "I can't stand it," she thought. "I'm turning around."

Our cat turned and quickly walked to Jennifer then raised her head to sniff her fingers.

Sniff…sniff…sniff…sniff…sniff.

"They smell so sweet!" our cat thought.

"Yes," the voice agreed.

Jennifer took a small step forward and carefully placed her hand on our cat's head then she slowly stroked it from front to back.

"She is deciding if she can trust you," the voice counseled. "People worry about cats biting and scratching them."

"Oh kitty…nice kitty cat…you're so sweet," Jennifer said with a soothing voice. "Are you the cat that lives in the storm drain? Where are you from? Are you all by yourself? Are you lost? Oh…you're such a nice kitty cat, aren't you kitty?"

The combination.

Our cat felt the nudge. She took a few more steps toward Jennifer then instinctively did what she did with Big Jim before he attacked her. She closed her eyes, cocked her head, twirled her tail, took a dip, butted her head on Jennifer's leg one time then rubbed her body against it.

"Again," the voice advised.

She turned around, found Jennifer's other leg then did it again.

"Oh kitty…you're so sweet!" Jennifer said. Our cat went back and forth from one leg to the next, dipping her head, rubbing her ears into Jennifer's legs. Jennifer was entranced. Then came the sound of love.

"Purr...purr...purr...purr...purr...purr...purr..."

"I am so happy," Jennifer said. "I love you kitty cat!" Jennifer was rubbing our cat's back, letting her move back and forth then weave between her legs.

The combination was working. Jennifer and our cat were creating love.

"Jennifer," Mom said with a welcoming voice from the top of the zoomway. "I see the kitty cat found you. That didn't take long."

Immediately, our cat wanted to flee.

"Stay," the voice encouraged. "You are a courageous cat."

It was hard to obey. She leaped away from Jennifer, walked to the middle of the street then turned to look at Mom.

"That's the cat from the storm drain," Mom said.

"Yes!" Jennifer said. "Oh Mom, she doesn't have a home, she's out here all by herself. You know she's hungry."

Mom walked to the bottom of the zoomway and acted just like Jennifer. She bent down, put her elbows on her legs, stretched out her hand then said, "Come here kitty... come here...come on...let me pet you kitty...come here." They looked like mother and daughter, coaxing our cat back to them.

"You have something they want," the voice said

"Love," our cat thought.

"Yes," the voice responded.

After a now instinctive pause, long enough to again establish petting was her idea, our cat walked slowly to Mom.

"Here she comes," Jennifer said with great anticipation.

Sniff, sniff, sniff, sniff, sniff.

"Mom smells like Jennifer," our cat thought.

"Yes," the voice agreed.

She closed her eyes, cocked her head, twirled her tail, took a dip, butted her head on Mom's leg one time then rubbed her body against it, only to keep going to Jennifer's leg where she did a 180, then back to Mom's leg.

"I am loving two of the people at the same time, and they are loving me!" she exclaimed to herself.

"Yes," the voice agreed.

She found a comfy spot next to Mom's leg.

"Purr...purr...purr...purr...purr...purr...purr..."

When Mom began rubbing her back, Jennifer was brainstorming the next move. "Mom, what can we give her?"

"Remember how the other night you left the milk in front of the garage and it was gone the next day?" Mom asked. "I'll bet it was her." Mom was rubbing our cat's back with a little more confidence.

"Milk" our cat thought. "Did I hear milk?"

"Yes," the voice said.

Our cat couldn't contain her excitement. She jumped off Mom's leg then began walking up the zoomway.

"She acts like she knows what we're going to do," Mom said.

Jennifer didn't care. She raced past our cat to the back of the house. Moments later she returned with a bowl of milk, carefully placing it in the same place as before, in front of the zoomway door, in front of her paw print.

"Are you hungry little kitty?" Mom said. "Do you want some milk?"

Our cat anxiously approached the bowl.

Lick, lick, lick, lick, lick, lick, lick, lick, lick, lick, lick, lick…

"Do you think she likes milk or what?" Mom asked, laughing.

"Oh mom, she's such as good cat," Jennifer said enthusiastically. Then, after pausing for what felt like an eternity, she blurted, "Can we keep her?"

"You know how your father feels about this cat," Mom apologized, sounding as if she wanted to keep our cat too. "He was pretty clear. He doesn't want a cat in the house."

Our cat was wagging her tail while devouring the milk. When she was close to finishing, Mom placed another bowl next to the milk, only this one was filled with food! Without missing a beat, she picked her head out of the milk bowl to take her first bite of real cat food.

Crunch, crunch, crunch, crunch, crunch, crunch, crunch, crunch...

"Mom," Jennifer exclaimed. "Where did you get the cat food?"

"I picked up a little bag at the store," Mom confessed.

As our cat enjoyed every morsel, something was happening behind her that quickly got her attention. She picked her head up out of the food bowl, looked toward the back of the tall house, and there, in the grass, was a short, squatty, thick, black, big pawed, dog. It was a miniature dachshund. Oh, oh...

The dog was enthusiastically sniffing the grass, and because the grass was tall and the dog so short, it had to jump in the air to get on to the zoomway.

"Jennifer, you shouldn't have let Puppy out," Mom cautioned.

"I didn't mean to," Jennifer said, "she just bolted through my legs when I was bringing out the milk."

"That damned dog," Mom said.

Puppy was walking toward Mom, wagging her tail, expecting to be petted, but then caught a glimpse of our cat. A black streak of hair immediately rose down the middle of her back from her neck to her tail. Then Puppy's fat little feet became flying flippers. Her long black toe nails made a clicking sound against the zoomway...her growl became a bark, bark, bark! She was attacking our cat!

But before our cat's feast could be interrupted, Mom stuck her foot out and gently kicked Puppy in the middle of her stomach. "CUT IT OUT PUPPY," Mom yelled.

As Puppy rolled over from Mom's blow, our cat became nervous. She knocked over the empty bowl of milk.

CLANG!

She ran to the bottom of zoomway but then stopped before getting to the street.

"Stay," said the voice. "You are a courageous cat."

Jennifer rushed to follow our cat down the zoom way. "Are you okay kitty cat? Are you okay?"

As Jennifer stopped to pet our cat, she closed her eyes again, cocked her head, twirled her tail, took a dip, butted her head on Jennifer's leg one time then rubbed her body against it.

Purr, purr, purr, purr, purr, purr, purr, purr, purr, purr, purr…

Puppy waddled around the zoomway, approached the cat food then started eating it.

"That's not your food!" Mom yelled. She took her hand and smacked Puppy's rear end. The defeated dog put her tail between here stubby legs then retreated to the back yard.

Soon Mom joined Jennifer at the bottom of the zoomway. "Are you okay, kitty cat?" Mom asked, "Are you okay?"

Instinctively our cat made a move toward Mom's leg, started rubbing her head against her, then began weaving back and forth, from this leg to that leg, from Mom back to Jennifer, then to Mom again. Both looked as if they couldn't move their feet.

Purr, purr, purr, purr, purr, purr, purr, purr, purr, purr, purr….

After a little more petting, Mom said, "Jennifer, your Dad's going to be home any minute. Don't tell him about the cat food."

"How come?" Jennifer asked.

"Your father doesn't want a cat in the house…and he knows what happens when you start feeding one. They don't go away."

Jennifer was confused. "You mean we can't keep her, but we can feed her and just let her live in that cold storm drain over there?" She was pointing toward it while waving her finger in the air.

"I don't know," Mom conceded. "Just don't tell your Dad. Okay?" Then, coming over the hill, was the tall man, Dad, in the zoom machine. "Here he comes. Remember what I said," Mom insisted.

As Mom and Jennifer walked back up the zoomway, our cat returned to the safety of her storm drain, but instead of going inside, she decided to sit on the brown round thing and pose.

As the zoom machine slowed to turn into the zoomway, Dad saw her. She turned her head away, looking toward the top of the hill, and noticed a familiar figure sitting there.

"That mean cat is watching me again," she exclaimed.

"Yes," the voice confirmed.

"I hate Big Jim," she insisted. But she didn't have much time to let anger build. After Dad parked his zoom machine in the zoom machine room, he walked down the zoomway and was coming right for her.

"WAAAA!" she said. She bounced off the brown round thing, did a fast 180 then crawled to her perch.

"Come on, cat," Dad begged. "Come out here. Let me pet you. Come on!"

Once again our cat would deny Dad from petting her, but this time it felt different. She watched Dad intently, but she was not terrified.

Dad said, "How come every time I try to pet a cat, I can't?" Frustrated, he turned and walked across the street, up the zoomway, to the zoom machine room. A moment later the big door came down, ending the excitement.

As the sunshine went away, you could hear our cat with a new ending line to her lullaby. "I'm so grateful and thankful for the abundance of food in the food field, I have a name, and I want to live with the people in the tall house before the Frosty Time comes, and in return I will give them love, *and they will love me.*"

Strategy 18

Make a combination.

When two things are combined they have a way of creating something new. Combining Jennifer and our cat created love!

Strategy 19

Give love.

When you give love, you are in the position to get love. When two love each other, a powerful bond is created and can grow into something magnificent.

When you think you have nothing to give, think again. You can give love!

Chapter 10: Repetition

Every morning Jennifer and Mom walk to the bottom of the zoomway. They wait until the big yellow zoom machine comes. When it pulls away, Jennifer will be gone, but Mom is always left behind.

"Cat," Mom will say, "Here kitty cat. Come on out here, kitty."

Without hesitation, our cat will emerge from the storm drain, walk across the street then follow Mom to the zoom machine door where she places clean bowls of milk and food in front of *her* paw print. When she starts licking the milk, Mom will affectionately rub her back.

"You're such a good cat," Mom will say.

The same thing happens in the afternoon. The big yellow zoom machine returns to drop Jennifer off. Then just like Mom in the morning, Jennifer will bring out more clean bowls of milk and food. Both girls pet our cat, talk to her, and give her love. In exchange, our cat gives them love back.

But then one day it turned freezing cold, and for some reason the big yellow zoom machine didn't come. Not knowing what was going on, our cat waited patiently, trying to stay warm. It was way past time to eat. Her stomach growled.

When she jumped out of the storm drain she was knocked over by the wind! Then the wind blew even harder. Leaves were swirling everywhere. One hit her face. It startled her. Branches on the trees were moving back and forth like crazy.

"What's happening?" she yelled.

"You have the answers to all my questions," she continued.

"The wind is blowing so hard I can't walk," she said. "Plus ... it's cold! It's really cold!"

She ran back into the storm drain.

"Whew," she exclaimed. "What is happening? Is THIS the beginning of Frosty Time?"

"Yes," the voice said.

Our cat balled up on her perch to keep warm. As she struggled to get comfortable she longingly looked across the street at her Dream Home. Looking at one of the windows in the top of the house she saw a light, and in the window staring back at her was Jennifer.

"She sees me," our cat said.

"Yes," the voice said.

The leaves continued to swirl, but they were joined by a new color.

"What are those white things floating everywhere?" she asked.

"Frozen tears," the voice said. "When it is this cold, tears from the sky turn white. They turn back to tears when it is warm."

"Look," she exclaimed, "they are sticking to the ground."

"Yes," the voice confirmed.

She watched the frozen tears swirling with the wind.

"I am hungry," she said. "I can go to the food field, but it is so cold! The mice are probably trying to stay warm too!"

As she watched the frozen tears dance in the air, something else caught her eye. "Look," she said. "There's Mom. She is next to Jennifer in the window."

Our cat got so excited she leaped out of the storm drain, but when her paws hit the slippery street she flopped on her side. The wind knocked her over, but that didn't stop her paws from moving. When she scrambled to her feet she took off fast. Instinctively she ran to the bottom of the zoomway hoping Jennifer and her Mom would see her, hoping they would come bring her food. It took all her strength to stay on her feet. The wind was extremely forceful making it feel much colder than the air in the storm drain.

"You are a courageous cat," the voice said.

It was difficult to pose. She began walking in a circle, keeping low to the ground, ears flopping, her fur flapping with the wind, frozen tears sticking to her. When she picked up her head and looked toward the top of the zoomway she saw Jennifer. She was fighting the wind, too.

"Kitty cat," she yelled as loudly as she could. "Come here, kitty cat!"

Our cat scurried up the zoomway and raced toward Jennifer who led her to the back of the Dream Home. "Come on kitty cat, come on in here," coaxed Jennifer through the wind. "I've got some food for you. See this blanket over my table? We're gonna try to keep you warm. So come on kitty cat, come on," she begged. Jennifer had made a temporary shelter on the deck just outside the back door.

"Should I go in there," she wondered. She was instinctively acting like it had to be her idea.

At that very moment the wind died down and the frozen tears were getting bigger, blanketing the wooden floor and her new temporary home. She noticed her fur was turning white.

"There's some milk in there for ya, girl" Jennifer coaxed. "You want some milk? Huh?"

Our cat bolted through the entrance to the newly created cavern. As Jennifer covered the opening with the blanket, it became almost dark inside. Her nose led her to the milk.

Lick, lick, lick, lick, lick, lick, lick, lick, lick, lick, lick, lick...

Jennifer placed a bowl of cat food in there, too.

Crunch, crunch, crunch, crunch, crunch, crunch, crunch, crunch...

Outside the cavern you could hear Mom. "Is the cat in there?" she asked loudly.

"It sure is, Mom," Jennifer shouted proudly. "She went right in."

"Come on sweetheart," Mom urged. "We gotta get inside. This storm is going to be big. Now don't tell your Dad what we're doing."

"Maaam," Jennifer whined as the two of them went inside the Dream Home. You could hear the frozen tears crunching under their feet. They slammed the door shut.

As the day wore on the wind came and went. The frozen tears never stopped. They grew so tall on the top and sides of the blanket it kept the cold out.

"I am so grateful...and so thankful...for the abundance of food from Jennifer," our cat exclaimed. "I love Jennifer!"

"Yes," the voice said.

Completely filled with milk, food, satisfied as she could possibly be despite the conditions, our cat was content. She curled up as tight as her fur would allow on a corner of the blanket, then fell asleep.

"I'm so grateful and thankful for the food in the food field...for the food from Jennifer ... purr ... purr ... I have...a...purr purr...name...purr...purr...purr."

Strategy 20

Repetition.

When you repeat something over and over again, the sum of the repetitions can make something stronger or even create something new.

Day after day, our cat used repetition as a strategy to get Jennifer and Mom to pet her and eventually love her. Now she is using repetition as a strategy to make their love stronger.

Strategy 21

Put yourself in the position to win.

If you want something, but you stay inside or don't go for it, you might miss out. The Law of Attraction is powerful, but opportunity rarely presents itself while you're glued to the perch of a storm drain or a comfy couch. Take action! Move those paws!

Chapter 11: Forgiveness

Inside Jennifer's temporary shelter was so dark it masked the arrival of sunshine and a new day. It came with so much warmth the frozen tears were disappearing.

"Everything is wet," our cat said.

"Yes," the voice confirmed. "Frozen tears are melting."

She carefully crept out of the shelter onto the wet wooden deck. Frozen tears were falling from the trees making a clean, crackling sound in the morning air. In front of her was the door to her Dream Home, the door where Mom and Jennifer come and go. Next to it the window she looked through where she first saw Jennifer. She jumped onto the window ledge then was immediately frightened.

"Who's that?" she exclaimed as she lunged off the ledge. "There's a cat in the window!"

She cocked her head to stare at it, looking for the cat, but it was gone.

"You are a courageous cat," the voice reminded her.

As our cat focused on the window, she realized she couldn't see inside the home; she couldn't see the people coming and going, the black dog named Puppy, or the green tree with the round things on it. Instead she saw sky and trees, so she jumped back on the ledge.

"There it is again!" our cat exclaimed, jumping to the safety of the wood floor.

"You…are seeing…you," the voice said.

"Me?" she asked quizzically.

"Yes," the voice said.

Our cat jumped to the ledge one more time. Sure enough, the cat in the window *was* her. It did everything she was doing.

"So that's me?" she asked. "That's what I look like?"

"Yes," the voice said.

She stared into her own eyes for the first time, getting so close her nose touched the window. Still trying to see inside, she could barely make out the green tree with the round things on it. Suddenly, Jennifer's face appeared.

"It's the cat, Mom!" she said enthusiastically from behind the glass.

Our cat leapt off the ledge one more time, but now there was an expectation stopping her from fleeing. FOOD! Jennifer opened the door, reached back inside, then emerged with a bowl of milk. She carefully placed it on the wood floor then pulled the door closed behind her.

Lick, lick, lick, lick, lick, lick, lick, lick, lick, lick, lick, lick…

Jennifer reached down to scratch the back of our cat's neck.

"You're so sweet, kitty," Jennifer said.

Jennifer pulled the soaking wet black blanket off the table, revealing two empty bowls. The door opened again. It was Mom.

"Looking for this?" she asked our cat. Mom placed another bowl next to the milk.

Crunch, crunch, crunch, crunch, crunch, crunch, crunch, crunch…

Mom reached down to scratch the back of her neck too. Our cat turned momentarily to glance at Mom, but immediately returned to devouring the cat food.

"What are we going to do, Mom?" Jennifer pined. "The big storm is coming, and she's out here all by herself."

"I don't know," Mom replied. "Let's not think about it right now."

"But Maaam," Jennifer continued. "Christmas is tomorrow."

"I know," Mom said. "Your Dad told me last night…*again*…he doesn't want a cat in the house. So for now, maybe we can put the table back up."

Jennifer and Mom kept talking as they went inside while our cat finished her food, strolled to the zoomway then turned toward the street. The sun was so brilliant it was almost blinding. As she walked by the zoom machine door, she saw her paw print. It made her feel good. But then, as she trotted down the zoomway she was shocked by the presence of a cat she never thought she'd confront ever again. There, at the bottom of the zoomway, blocking the path to her storm drain was Big JIM!

She stopped to stare.

"You are a courageous cat," the voice said.

Keeping her distance, our cat demanded "What are *you* doing here?" Our cat looked him over, but for some reason Big Jim didn't look so big anymore. He was looking more like a regular cat, but with a big question mark on his face. She crept closer.

In a soft voice, Big Jim said meekly, "I want to talk to you."

"I can't hear you," said our cat firmly.

"I want to talk to you," Jim asked a little louder.

She felt a nudge. She approached Big Jim without fear.

"Sure," she said, filling with confidence.

"The people," Big Jim said. "Ever since the day you came for help…"

"You mean ever since the day you almost killed me," she interrupted.

"Yes," Big Jim said apologetically. "They've stopped treating me special, like they've stopped loving me. Treats are gone. They don't pet me like they used to. There are even times my door gets locked while I'm still outside. It's like they don't care about me anymore."

"Keep going," she said.

"All I know is when they saw me hurt you, something changed," Big Jim said. "It was like I hurt myself, too."

Our cat drew even closer, so close that Big Jim could have taken a swipe at her face. But that wasn't happening. Not this time. Something was different.

"Okay," our cat said. "What are you saying?"

"Something came over me when I opened my eyes and you were in my face," Big Jim confessed. "Maybe I was selfish, not wanting to share you with my people. Maybe I just snapped. I don't have an excuse. I...am...sorry."

"I think about you a lot," she said. "How you whacked my face with your claws, how you jumped me, then bit me so hard on my back. You hurt me."

"I am sorry," Big Jim repeated.

"And why," she continued, "why does a cat like you who almost killed me, get the good life, get to live with the people, people who give you food, a place to live, even a door with your name on it, while I live in the storm drain over there?" She motioned with her head across the street.

Big Jim humbly said, "Things have changed, they're not as good as they used to be." Then he asked her a huge question.

"Will you forgive me," he said.

Our cat returned a blank stare. "What do you mean forgive you?" she asked curiously. She didn't understand what he was asking.

The cats sat and stared at each other for what seemed like an eternity, but then Big Jim made a move. He stood, walked toward our cat, closed his eyes, turned his head, dipped his shoulder then rubbed his body against hers. As Big Jim finished rubbing in one direction, he turned to do it again. She melted. Then, as he went back for another pass, he stopped, gazed into her eyes, dropped his head then repeated, "Will you forgive me?"

The combination of affection and the confession was having an impact on our cat. She was feeling good.

"Every time I thought about you, I felt bad," Big Jim confessed. "I felt bad because I knew you felt bad about me. I don't want to feel bad anymore. From now on, when I think about you I want to feel good."

"You know," she confided, "Every time I thought about you, I felt bad, too. How is it possible, how is it fair, knowing that I did nothing wrong?"

"So will you?" he asked. "Will you put this in the past? Will you forgive me?"

Our cat stared at Big Jim, intently listening for the voice, but it was silent. She remembered how the voice taught her about being the leader, and how making decisions was her job. Then she made a sound, the same sound her voice has been making in her head.

"Yes," she said. "I forgive you."

She still didn't completely understand what she just did, but a new feeling came over her like sunshine melting away frozen tears. "Why do I suddenly feel good?" she asked.

Big Jim didn't respond. He was relieved to hear her words of forgiveness...words of relief. His eyes filled with gratitude. He closed them then began rubbing against our cat again and again and again. He was feeling good, too.

"All right Jim, all right" our cat said, almost embarrassingly.

Jim stopped to sit and stare at her face. Then he asked the other question he came for. "Will you come to my house? Will you let the people see us together? If the people see you with me, well...uh..."

"Well...uh...what Jim? What?" she teased.

The nervous black and white cat said, "That...well...if we figured out a way to like each other...or...or maybe...love each other...then if they saw us...together...they could see you have forgiven me. Then maybe...just maybe...the people would forgive me too."

Feral cats are not accustomed to this much love and affection. Instinctively she stood. "Let's go," she said.

Big Jim leaped in the air to lead the charge up the hill. As they trotted side-by-side our cat began to realize he could help her understand the people *she* was trying to live with. She loves Jennifer and Mom, but is still afraid of the tall man.

"I saw the man and the woman at your house," she said. "Are you afraid of the man?" she asked.

"The man is great," Big Jim said. "He feeds me, cleans my kitty litter, and scratches my back."

As they trotted into Big Jim's yard she saw the woman, the same woman that chased Jim off her back. She turned toward the zoom machine room and excitedly yelled, "John...John come quick!" The man came up next to her in the zoomway. "It's the little cat Jim had the fight with," she said. "I never thought we'd see her again."

"I know it, Pam," John said as he walked toward them. "It doesn't make any sense at all. I thought we had a mean, big 'ol selfish cat here, but maybe we were wrong. Maybe our Jim is a lovable kitty after all."

As Big Jim ran toward John's legs and curled around them our cat cautiously approached Pam. The woman stuck her hand out. Our cat looked away for a moment, remembering all this has to be her idea, then stepped into her fingers...

Sniff, sniff, sniff, sniff...

Our cat closed her eyes, stepped forward to head butt one of Pam's legs, and then began lovingly rubbing and weaving around them.

"John, she is so sweet," Pam said. "I wonder if she has a home."

"Paaam," John cautioned, "We don't want another cat now. Do we?"

Big Jim looked toward our cat and said, "If you let John pet you, maybe you won't be so afraid of your tall man."

Our cat brushed Pam's leg one more time, stuck her left paw out to stretch then made the move toward John. He put out his hand; she sniffed it a couple of times. The man reached behind her neck and started to scratch it. She was in heaven.

"See," Jim confirmed, "the man is great."

She moved to rub and weave between John's legs then decided it would be okay to let the tall man pet her.

"Let's play," Big Jim said.

"Thank you," she replied as she received a nudge from the voice, "but it's time for me to go."

She jumped away from John, ran down the zoomway then began quickly walking up the hill. When she made it to the top, she turned to see Big Jim. He was watching her from the end of his zoomway. He had a *big* smile on his face.

Forgiveness.

Our cat paused to sit on the top of the hill to stare at Big Jim. "So that was forgiveness?" she asked.

"Yes," the voice said.

She began kneading her paws into the sidewalk.

"What does it mean?" she asked.

"I have the answers for all of your questions," the voice said.

"You have been living with anger for what Big Jim did to you, and envy because you accepted Negative Nancy's suggestion. These are both bad emotions. When you allow anger and envy to take over your thoughts, *you* feel bad."

"When you think bad thoughts," she said, "bad things happen."

"Yes," the voice said.

"When you think good thoughts," she continued, "and when you feel good, good things happen."

"Yes," the voice repeated. "Forgiveness means letting go completely, so when you forgave Jim, you let your feelings of hate and envy go, too. That's why you feel good."

Our cat spread her shoulders then stuck her tail straight into the air.

"Your act of kindness; your decision of forgiveness let the people forgive Jim too," the voice said. "That means the people feel good, Big Jim feels good…and *YOU* feel good. Now comes the good part."

"There's more?" she asked.

"Yes," the voice said. "Repeat your purpose."

"I am so grateful and thankful I am living with the people in my Dream Home before Frosty Time comes, and in return I will give them love," she said.

"Listen to me," the voice said. "This will be one of the most important things you learn."

Our cat stood to see her Dream Home. As she sat to listen to the voice, she recognized the tall man sitting at the bottom of his zoomway.

"You love Jennifer and Mom," the voice said, "and they love you. Now you can give them all of your love."

"I have more love to give?" she asked.

"Yes," the voice said. "It is impossible to feel love and hate at the same time. It is impossible to feel both unconditional love *and* envy. You can only have one feeling at a time. By removing the hate, by removing the envy, you make room for the only feeling left to give…love! Yes, you have more love to give, the kind of love when you give it, and get it back, it lasts forever."

"I can love the tall man, too," she said.

"Yes," the voice said.

She felt a nudge. She stood, then started trotting down the hill, taking an angle straight for the tall man. He saw her.

"Here she comes," he cheered. "Here cat, hey kitty, come here kitty cat, come here."

She waltzed across the street to the bottom of the zoomway. The man was sitting with his elbows on knees, waiting to see what she would do.

"Come here," he coaxed. "Do you wanna sniff my hand?"

As our cat approached the tall man she paused, sat down then looked away.

"Are you going to make me beg?" he complained. "Sheesh! Get over here."

She turned to look back toward the man, started kneading her paws, stood, took two steps then let her nose touch his fingers.

Sniff, sniff, sniff, sniff.

The tall man wasn't budging. He was waiting for her to make the first move…and she did. She took two steps closer so he could scratch the back of her head. When he did, she started wagging her tail side to side. Then she went under one of his legs and rubbed it, only to return to do it again.

"You're a good cat," the man said. As she was moving away from his leg she looked up and saw Mom walking down the zoomway.

"So you FINALLY got to pet the cat," Mom said.

"Yea," Dad said. "Too bad she lives in the storm drain. Now…you know I don't really want a cat, 'cause nobody else I'm related to will take care of it. I'd be the one cleaning the kitty litter, feeding it, and…"

"Oh, come on," Mom interrupted. "She would be fine. Jennifer and I can take care of it."

"Yea, whatever." Dad wasn't buying the claim.

"Look how dark the sky is over there," Mom said, pointing over the top of the Dream Home. "We're going to get slammed with that ice storm tonight."

"Well...what about the cat?" Dad asked.

"Well...what about the cat?" Mom quipped. "You made it clear you didn't want a cat."

"I know," he conceded.

"Look," Mom said, "it's Christmas Eve, bad weather is coming, we'll figure out something."

When Dad stood up, he frightened our cat. She dashed to the middle of the street then crawled in the storm drain.

"Another storm?" our cat asked.

"Yes," the voice said. "Frosty Time is definitely here."

Strategy 22

Forgiveness.

When you have been wronged, slighted, hurt, or stolen from, it's hard to assume innocence, to let it go. It is much easier, more common, to get mad, and eventually get even.

But what that means is despite doing absolutely nothing wrong, now *you* are the one with the bad, negative feelings. When you feel bad, when you think negative things, you get negative things.

When you discover the power of forgiveness, especially the first time, you will be surprised how liberated you will feel. The more you do it, the more you let go, the more your mind is dominated by positive things ... positive thoughts…positive ideas.

When you think good thoughts, you get good things. SO LET IT GO!

Chapter 12: Receive

KAAAABOOOOOOOOOMMMMM!

A loud clap, bright light, then rumbling thunder shook the neighborhood. The sound of huge wind gusts became background noise to the roar of tears coming from the sky. It didn't take a moment for tears landing in the street to find their way to the slit of the storm drain. When they fell to the floor of the drain it was almost deafening.

As our cat tried to get a glimpse of her Dream Home through the darkness and tears, she noticed the sides of the storm drain were closing in; the slit was shrinking. Her home was transforming into a death trap.

"What is happening to the slit?" asked our frantic cat.

"Hard tears," the voice said.

"Can the hard tears trap me in here?" she asked.

"Yes," the voice said.

"If I get trapped in here, can the rats eat me?" she asked.

"Yes," the voice confirmed.

Faith.

As she sits on her perch, and the slit slowly narrows, she has no fear.

"You are filled with love," the voice said, "so much love you have created faith, faith in yourself, and faith that your purpose is being fulfilled."

Our cat stood on her perch for the last time. She paused to remember the nights she spent there, how she used to be hungry, how she was so lonely, how she put up with living with the rat. Now she is making a decision. A decision to put her in the position for a better life, a life filled with abundance, a life living with the people in her Dream Home. She coiled up, aimed for the shrinking hole, then bolted from the storm drain forever.

SPLAT!

She slipped, fell on her side, then started sliding down the hill. She desperately clawed the air, but got no traction. Her fur was quickly covered with tears turning hard. But then … luckily … she stopped sliding. When she looked up the hill, she could see she had gone a long way. The hard tears on her fur were getting bigger.

"How will I get up the hill to the zoomway?" she asked. "How will I make it there?"

As she looked longingly toward her Dream Home, she got a nudge. She picked up her right front paw and extended her claws. Then she got her idea. CLAWS!

Our cat unleashed claws from all four paws, then step-by-step, cautiously crept up the hill to the mouth of the zoomway. Being careful not to slip for fear of sliding back down the hill, she stopped to look at the house. All the windows were glowing, but she couldn't see any of the people.

"They must be in the back," she thought.

Fighting the wind, struggling with the growing weight of the hard tears on her back, she extended her claws one more time, then raced up the zoomway, passed the zoomway door with her paw print, then scurried to the back of the house. The makeshift cavern was waiting for her. She darted up the steps of the wooden deck, found the opening of the blanket, then slipped inside.

"All these hard tears on my fur are making me so cold," she said.

She sniffed around and found her bowl of milk, but it was frozen! Then, the wind blew with such amazing force it picked her cavern up and threw it into the yard! The relentless tears hit her face and little body with incredible intensity. She could hardly see.

"The ledge," the voice said. "Jump to the ledge."

Without hesitation she coiled then jumped onto the ledge, the ledge of the window where she could look inside to see the people.

JUMP...SPLAT!

She was so heavy from the hard tears on her back she fell short.

"Try again," the voice encouraged.

She coiled herself again, jumped as high as she could then just as she got there extended her claws to grip the ledge.

"I made it!" she exclaimed.

"The window is so warm…and I am so cold," she said. "Jennifer, Jennifer, can you hear me Jennifer? JENNIFERRRRR!"

She was meowing at the top of her lungs, hoping Jennifer would hear her, AND SHE DID!

"Mom…Dad…look!" exclaimed Jennifer on the other side of window. "It's Kitty! She's freezing! Help her Mom, help her Dad! Can we let her in? Please? Oh…my gosh ... "

As the people drew close to the window, our cat looked vulnerable, helpless, and pathetic. The scene was so compelling, it moved the family to take action.

Jennifer ran to the door. Mom was right behind her. As it opened, our cat heard the sweetest sound she has ever heard in her life, *her name.*

"Kitty!" yelled Mom. "Get in here!"

Kitty jumped off the window and darted into her Dream Home. The door behind her slammed shut. She was inside!

"Mom, get a towel," Jennifer begged. "Kitty...oh Kitty...are you okay?"

Mom brought a towel to Kitty, picked her up and put her on top of a counter, then rubbed her with the towel. The hard tears began to melt and fall off her fur. Dry enough, she jumped off the counter to walk into the room with the green tree.

Oh oh...there was that dog again.

"Puppy," Jennifer cautioned, "don't even *think* about it!"

As Puppy cowered away, Kitty sensed she was surrounded by all four of the people.

"Kitty, this is your new home," Jennifer said. "I named you Kitty, and that's what we're going to call you. This is my Mom, this is my Dad, and this is my little brother Phill."

Kitty was crouched low, looking around the room. Everything was so warm and filled with joy. She shook her head then her entire body to throw off the tears left on her fur. Not knowing where to go or what to do, she saw the green tree with the round things and ran behind it.

Jennifer followed her to the tree, got on her knees then stretched out one of her hands.

"Here Kitty," Jennifer coaxed. "Come here sweetheart." As Kitty slowly crept from behind the tree, Jennifer began scratching the back of her neck. Kitty loved it so much she soon fell to her side to let Jennifer scratch her back, when she did, Kitty reached out with her front claws to grab the carpet while stretching her back legs and rolling her eyes.

"Phill," Mom instructed, "get that kitty litter set up in the wash room. Jennifer, get her food bowl out and fill it up."

After the kids went to work, Mom took Jennifer's place with Kitty in front of the green tree, got down on her knees then said, "Welcome home, Kitty. Merry Christmas!"

Kitty received her miracle. She was living with the people in her Dream Home, and Frosty Time had just started. In return, she was giving them love.

Tears of joy.

Jennifer was in the wash room of the Dream Home. It was right next to the kitchen. "Here Kitty, here Kitty, come to your new home."

Kitty scurried out of the room with the green tree, crept half way across the kitchen floor, then darted into the wash room.

"Come on up here girl," Jennifer said. Jennifer was patting the counter top with her hand.

Kitty coiled her little body, now completely dry from the tears, then leapt up onto the counter. Jennifer had already placed her new, comfy bed directly in front of the window. It was perfectly positioned so she could look outside to the backyard. Next to it was fresh cat food and milk.

"This is your bed, Kitty," Jennifer said. "Here's your milk bowl, and see on your food bowl? That's your name on it. Kitty!"

Kitty remembered Big Jim's name on the zoomway door, her paw print outside on her zoomway door, then got excited. It was all sinking in. Everything she dreamed about was happening!

"This is your place to live," Jennifer said. Kitty tip-toed into her bed. Then Jennifer started stroking her back.

"Santa is coming tonight," she said, "so I have to go to bed. This is going to be your room for a while, girl. I'm going to close the door so the dogs don't bother you."

Kitty was exhausted. There had been so much excitement that she was ready to go to sleep, too. As Jennifer closed the door, she left a little light on in the room. Kitty stood in her bed, did a 360, then flopped back down and stared out the window.

"There I am," Kitty said, looking into the window, remembering how she could see herself, but then her reflection began to glow, glowing just like she did when Big Cat saved her life. Glowing like she did when she discovered her purpose.

"Yes," the voice said. "Here I am. I…am…you."

Kitty began to realize the cat looking back at her looked just like her, but it wasn't her.

"I can see you," Kitty said.

"Yes," the voice said, staring back at her.

"You are me," Kitty agreed.

"Yes," the voice encouragingly said. "I…am…you."

"You're glowing," Kitty said. "That means something."

"Yes," the voice agreed. "We're going back to the way it is supposed to be."

"Will you still hear me?" Kitty asked.

"Yes," the voice said, "because I…am…you."

"Will you answer my questions?" Kitty asked.

 "I have the answers for all of your questions," the voice said.

"How will I understand what you are telling me?" Kitty asked.

"When you feel a nudge," the voice said. "When an idea comes to you, or you hear what sounds like a little voice, that will be me…you'll know it!"

As Kitty listened passionately to her voice, she noticed the glow in the window was slowly fading. The voice…was disappearing.

"I am so happy…and sad…all at the same time," she cried.

"You can only have one feeling at a time," the voice said.

"My feeling…is joy," Kitty exclaimed as tears rolled from her eyes.

And just like *every* time before…the voice answered, "Yes."

Soon…the glow faded…and then…it was gone. The voice…disappeared. All that remained…all Kitty could see, was her own faint reflection.

Gratitude.

Kitty bowed her head, closed her eyes then said, "I am so grateful and thankful I have a name, am here in my Dream Home, with the people, Mom, Dad, Jennifer, Phill, and I am so grateful and thankful it happened before Frosty Time. Thank you…thank you Big Cat… thank you…"

Purr, purr, purr, purr, purr, purr.

Chapter 13: Strategies for Cats (and People)

"Self-help" books solve problems. If you're a cat and you're homeless (a problem), Strategies for Cats will help you find a home before Frosty Time comes (a solution). But unless you're a homeless cat, how do *you* benefit from the 22 Strategies for Cats? What new power do *you* possess?

Change the Way You Think.

The voice told Kitty, "Whatever you think about the most is what I bring into your life. That means you are responsible for everything happening in your life right now, the food, the cold, the rat, staying away from people, living a storm drain…all are the things you think about."

Kitty became dejected, then asked, "What you're saying is all these things are the way they are now because of the way I think?"

The voice answered like it always answers. "**_Yes_.** You have attracted all of these things into your life."

This was the turning point in the story for Kitty!

She became dejected, dropped her head and slouched her shoulders, but then she remembered her feel good thought. She realized having the power to control her thoughts so she can think good thoughts versus bad thoughts means she has the power to change her life forever.

The Cause of Kitty's Problem.

Being homeless and living in a storm drain was a problem. What was the cause of that problem? The way she was thinking.

The Cause of Your Problems.

Having a mound of debt in your life is a problem. What is the cause of that problem? The way you think.

Not having the love of your life *in* your life is a problem. What is the cause of that problem? The way you think.

Missing out on the promotion you wanted…again…is a problem. What is the cause of that problem? The way you think.

Having a car that always breaks down, is never reliable, embarrassing for you to drive, is a problem. What is the cause of that problem? The way you think.

Being unhappy all the time is a problem. What is the cause of that problem? The way you think.

Bad things seem to always happen to you all the time! What is the cause of that problem? *The way you think.*

The cause of every problem in your life begins with the way you think. Change the way you think, believe your thoughts become things, and now you have the power to solve every problem in your life right now!

Team up with Your Voice.

Receive the Abundance You Deserve.

Having a mound of money in your life is a solution to a problem. How can you manifest that mound of money into your life? By teaming up with your subconscious mind…and changing the way you think.

Meeting the love of your life is a solution. How can you manifest the love of your life into your life? By teaming up with your subconscious mind…and changing the way you think.

Getting the promotion you've always wanted is a solution. How can you manifest that promotion into your life? By teaming up with your subconscious mind…and changing the way you think.

Driving the brand new car, truck or SUV of your dreams is a solution! How can you manifest that new vehicle into your life? By teaming up with your subconscious mind…and changing the way you think.

Being happy all the time, staying away from Negative Nancy, is a solution. How can you manifest happiness into your life? By teaming up with your subconscious mind…and changing the way you think.

Good things seem to always happen to you all the time. You're lucky! How can you manifest all those good things into your life? By teaming up with your subconscious mind…and changing the way you think.

It takes an effort to change the way you think…but when you do…you will receive the abundance you deserve!

Cats and People Who Have Used the Power of their Subconscious Mind.

When you decide to change the way you think, and receive the abundance you deserve, add your name to this list of famous cats and people known to have used the power of their subconscious mind and the Law of Attraction to answer the most impossible questions, to solve the biggest problems in their lives and the lives of others, and to receive the abundance they deserved!

Thomas Edison

Henry Ford

Albert Einstein

Guglielmo Marconi

Dr. Martin Luther King, Jr.

Winston Churchill

Maya Angelou

Abraham Lincoln

Anne Frank

Shakespeare

Helen Keller

Mark Twain

Andrew Carnegie

Kitty

Ralph Waldo Emerson

Walt Whitman

Walt Disney

Napoleon Hill

You *(write your name here):*

_____

About the Author

Bill A Johnston was born and raised in Jamestown NY in 1955, grew up in the perfect family, graduated from Jamestown High School in 1973, Jamestown Community College in 1975, and Syracuse University with a Bachelors in Television and Radio from the Newhouse School of Communications in 1977.

For more than twenty-five years, Bill has been operating radio stations in the Carolinas, including writing and voicing radio ads using his distinctive and immediately recognizable voice. He also created the Answers! CD in 2002-2003, publishing more than 1.5 million copies to the cable television industry, as well as wrote and produced film-based ads that ran nationally. Today he is President of Now Mobile Media, in business since 2000. In addition, he is pursuing his purpose as a professional speaker, and has written this book, Strategies for Cats.

When you read his book or hear him speak, Bill is committed to helping you "change the way you think," so you can "receive the abundance you deserve." He enjoys working and speaking with companies in need of creating new thinking, new energy, new ideas, and new directions.

Bill has been married to his beautiful wife Cecelia for more than thirty-six years, and has two children, a son-in-law, and four grandchildren. As Zig Ziglar said, "If I knew I wanted grand-children this bad, I would have been nicer to their parents!"

Bill lives in Burlington, North Carolina. Kitty lives there too! To contact Bill for speaking engagements, visit: http://www.billajohnston.com.

A Special Bonus from Bill

I am so thankful and grateful you have a copy of Strategies for Cats! It is my sincere hope that, by reading this book, you change the way you think so you can receive the abundance you deserve!

To express my gratitude, I'd like to give you a free, beautiful PDF featuring the 22 Strategies for Cats. It's a convenient and easy way to review and remember all the Strategies, and perfect for your refrigerator door!

To receive your free copy of the 22 Strategies for Cats suitable for framing, please visit our website:

http://www.strategiesforcats.com/bookbonus

To contact me for speaking engagements on Strategies for Cats, visit:

http://www.billajohnston.com

Plus, for even more on the book, the adventures of Kitty, and me, visit and <u>like</u> our Facebook page:

http://www.facebook.com/strategiesforcats

31074987R00088

Made in the USA
Middletown, DE
18 April 2016